Welcome to Web3: A Multi-Level Introduction to the Decentralized Internet

Welcome to *Web3*, an authoritative PhD-level textbook that explores the new decentralized internet revolution. This book is structured to guide **multiple audiences** – from newcomers to seasoned professionals – through the multifaceted world of Web3. It delves deep into technical, economic, and social dimensions of blockchain networks, decentralized autonomous organizations (DAOs), smart contracts, decentralized finance (DeFi), artificial intelligence (AI) integration, and even quantum computing's role in the future of Web3. Each chapter is carefully organized with sections tailored for **beginners**, **intermediate learners**, **advanced professionals**, and **researchers**, so you can progress through the material at the level of detail that suits you best. We also include extensive **case studies**, rigorous **mathematical and algorithmic insights**, interdisciplinary analyses, practical **hands-on guides**, thought-provoking **exercises**, and a rich historical and philosophical context to ground your understanding. Throughout the book, you'll find citations to cutting-edge research (including the seminal works of Dr. Justin Goldston and others) to back key points. By the end, you'll not only grasp the "what" and "how" of Web3 technologies, but also the "why" – the broader implications for society, governance, and the future. Let's embark on this journey into the decentralized frontier.

Introduction and How to Use This Book

Web3 refers to the third generation of internet services, defined by decentralization, blockchain-based technologies, and token-driven economics ted.com. Unlike the current Web2 (dominated by centralized platforms), Web3 aims to give control back to users through distributed networks, cryptography, and community governance. This introductory chapter will set the stage for what Web3 is and how this textbook is structured to accommodate different readers.

What is Web3? *(Beginner)*

In simple terms, Web3 is the idea of a new, decentralized internet built on blockchains (public ledgers maintained by a network of computers rather than a central server). In Web3:

- **Users Own Their Data:** Instead of big companies owning your personal data or content, ownership is secured by cryptography on public blockchains.
- **Peer-to-Peer Transactions:** Cryptocurrencies enable value exchange on the internet without banks or intermediaries.
- **Decentralized Applications (dApps):** Applications run on networks like Ethereum, where no single entity controls the app – the community does, via tokens and smart contracts.

For a beginner, think of Web3 as an **internet by the people, for the people**, where communities collectively run platforms (social networks, financial apps, games, etc.), and rules are enforced by code (smart contracts) rather than corporate policies.

Multi-Audience Roadmap *(All Levels)*

This book explicitly caters to a **multi-audience** readership. Each chapter is divided into sections marked for different knowledge levels:

- **Beginner:** Introduces concepts in an accessible way, assuming little to no prior knowledge. These sections explain

terminology and basic ideas with real-life analogies or simple examples.
- **Intermediate:** Explores technical details and practical aspects. These sections may assume you understand the basics and are ready to learn how things work under the hood (for example, how blockchain transactions are processed or how to write a simple smart contract).
- **Advanced Professional:** Dives into complex mechanisms, optimizations, and issues relevant to experts in the field. Here you'll find in-depth discussions of algorithms, protocols, cryptographic techniques, and system architectures. Mathematical models and proofs may appear to solidify understanding of security and performance.
- **Researcher:** Examines open problems, cutting-edge research, and interdisciplinary perspectives. These sections connect you with the latest academic work and theoretical frameworks (including Dr. Justin Goldston's Web3 Systems Thinking Theory) to inspire further inquiry thinkers360.com. Expect references to scholarly papers, experimental technologies (like quantum-resistant cryptography), and thought experiments about the future of Web3.

How to read this book: If you're new to Web3, focus on the **Beginner** sections in each chapter to build a foundation, and use the Intermediate sections as your next step. If you have some background, you might skim the beginner parts and dive into **Intermediate** and **Advanced** discussions. Researchers and advanced professionals can jump straight to the **Advanced** and **Researcher** sections for each topic, where we provide rigorous analysis and cite current research. Feel free to mix-and-match – the book is designed so you can get value at any depth of knowledge. Each chapter ends with **Exercises and Discussion Questions** to test your understanding and encourage deeper reflection or hands-on practice.

Now, let's start our exploration by looking at where Web3 comes from – the history of decentralization and how we arrived at this point.

The History and Philosophy of Decentralization *(Beginner to Researcher)*

Before diving into technology, it's important to understand the historical and philosophical context that gave birth to Web3. The desire for decentralization has roots in both technological evolution and human ideals of liberty and trust. In this chapter, we trace the journey from the early internet to today's Web3 movement, and link these developments to key scholarly works, including Dr. Justin Goldston's research on hybrid finance, digital inheritance, the metaverse, and digital identity.

From Web 1.0 to Web3: Evolution of the Internet *(Beginner)*

The internet has gone through major eras:

- **Web 1.0 (1990s):** Mostly read-only, static websites. This early web was decentralized in that anyone could host a website, but interaction was limited.
- **Web 2.0 (2000s–2020s):** The interactive, social web. Platforms like Facebook, YouTube, and Twitter enabled user-generated content and global communication. However, Web2 became highly **centralized** – a few big tech companies control social media, e-commerce, and other services. Users trade control for convenience, giving platforms power over data and content.
- **Web3 (emerging now):** A response to Web2's centralization. Web3 uses **blockchain technology** (introduced by Bitcoin in 2008) to create networks where no

single party is in charge. Trust is placed in **mathematics and code** (e.g. cryptography, consensus algorithms) rather than corporations or governments. This enables **trustless** interactions: you don't need to know or trust the other party or a middleman when the system's rules (smart contracts) automatically enforce fairness.

The term *Web3* itself was popularized to mean an internet that is decentralized, permissionless (anyone can participate without authorization), and based on **token economics** (digital assets that incentivize network participation). It's an internet where communities can create their own self-governed online organizations and economies.

The Roots of Decentralization *(Intermediate)*

Decentralization is not a new idea – it underpins many aspects of computer networks and political philosophy:

- In the 1970s-80s, the internet's precursor (ARPANET) was designed as a decentralized network to survive outages. Peer-to-peer protocols (like BitTorrent for file sharing or the Tor network for anonymous communication) continued this ethos of distributed power.
- The **Cypherpunk movement** (1990s) comprised activists who advocated using cryptography to achieve privacy and freedom in the digital age. It produced innovations like PGP encryption and foreshadowed cryptocurrencies. In 2008, Satoshi Nakamoto released the Bitcoin whitepaper, introducing a blockchain-based digital currency that didn't require any bank – a purely peer-to-peer form of electronic cash. Bitcoin's success demonstrated that **distributed consensus** at scale was possible, solving the "double-spending problem" without a central authority through a clever Proof-of-Work algorithm.
- Early cryptocurrencies were followed by platforms like Ethereum (2015), which generalized the idea with **smart**

contracts (self-executing code on the blockchain) to support a variety of decentralized applications. This enabled concepts like *decentralized finance* (DeFi) and *decentralized autonomous organizations* (DAOs) to flourish by 2020.

From a philosophical standpoint, decentralization resonates with the desire for **self-sovereignty** – the idea that individuals should control their own identity, assets, and destiny without undue reliance on centralized institutions. This connects to political philosophies (e.g., libertarian ideals of limited government, or the notion of digital commonwealths) and even deeper human themes of trust and power distribution.

Decentralization and the Cycles of Control (Advanced)

History shows a pendulum between **centralization** and **decentralization**. In technology and economics, centralized systems can be very efficient (consider how Web2 companies build powerful, optimized services), but they can become monopolistic and fragile (single points of failure, or potential for abuse of power). Decentralized systems prioritize resilience and trust through transparency and redundancy, at the cost of some efficiency or convenience.

Systems thinking tells us to look at the whole: A decentralized network (like a blockchain) is a complex adaptive system involving technology, incentives, and human participants. Dr. Justin Goldston's *Web3 Systems Thinking Theory* proposes that to truly understand Web3, one must integrate perspectives from technology, economics, law, governance, and more. We will revisit this in a later chapter, but even historically, we see this interplay:

- The success of a decentralized currency (Bitcoin) was not just a technical milestone but an economic experiment challenging central bank models.

- The rise of DAOs to coordinate people via tokens harks back to cooperative organizations and even social contracts in political theory.
- The push-pull with regulators (e.g., governments trying to apply existing laws to borderless, decentralized networks) is a theme that began as soon as Napster and BitTorrent tested intellectual property law, and continues with today's debates over cryptocurrency regulation.

Key Point: Web3's emergence is as much a social phenomenon as a technological one. It's born from dissatisfaction with Web2's concentration of power and fueled by advances in cryptography and computing. Understanding this context will help you appreciate why certain design decisions (like emphasizing transparency, or community governance) are so important in Web3 projects.

A Philosophical Perspective: Digital Identity, Legacy, and Society *(Advanced)*

Decentralization isn't just about technology – it's also about reimagining concepts like identity and legacy in the digital realm:

- In Web2, your digital identity (accounts, profiles) is ultimately controlled by companies. Web3 introduces **Self-Sovereign Identity (SSI)** – you own verifiable credentials and reputation tokens that you carry independent of any platform. For example, **Soulbound Tokens** (a concept proposed by Ethereum's Vitalik Buterin and examined by Dr. Goldston et al.) are non-transferable tokens that could represent personal achievements or characteristics, forming a digital resume of sorts that no one can take away from you articlegateway.com.
- With the accumulation of digital assets (cryptocurrencies, NFTs), there's a new question: what happens to these when one dies? Traditional inheritance law struggles with secret cryptographic keys. This led to research on **digital inheritance** in Web3. Goldston and collaborators (2023)

proposed frameworks using soulbound tokens and **social recovery** mechanisms to pass on assets securely arxiv.org. (Social recovery means you can designate trusted contacts who can help recover your wallet if you're incapacitated, without any one person controlling it – a decentralized twist on a will.)
- Philosophically, some have begun to view persistent digital identities and assets as a way to achieve a form of immortality or lasting legacy. Goldston's study applied **Terror-Management Theory** (a psychology theory about fear of death) to Web3, suggesting that people accumulate NFTs and tokens partly to create a legacy that lives on after them articlegateway.com. In this sense, decentralization touches on existential questions: if your online persona and creations are immortal on the blockchain, what does that mean for how we find meaning? The same study looked at NFTs as "proof-of-ownership" and soulbound tokens as "proof-of-character," indicating how Web3 might evolve into a *Decentralized Society* where reputation and value are encoded on-chain articlegateway.com.
- Another angle is the concept of the **Metaverse** – a persistent virtual world. While not all metaverse ideas are decentralized (Facebook's "Meta" is a corporate effort), the Web3 vision is a **decentralized metaverse** where users own land, avatars, and assets as NFTs, and governance is by the community. Goldston's case study *"The Metaverse as the Digital Leviathan"* examined *Bit.Country*, a metaverse on Polkadot, through the lens of philosopher Thomas Hobbes' *Leviathan*. It considered whether decentralized virtual worlds might start to resemble "Leviathans" – powerful states – and concluded that good governance (a "quadruple bottom line" balancing economic, social, environmental, and existential goals) is essential to keep a metaverse both prosperous and ruled by the people rather than by corporate kings articlegateway.com. This implies that history may repeat: even in new digital frontiers, we must be vigilant to ensure

decentralization truly empowers users and doesn't just create new forms of concentration.

In summary, the push for decentralization in Web3 is deeply rooted in historical trends and philosophical ideals:

- It's a reaction to the centralization of Web2.
- It extends longstanding efforts to use technology for individual empowerment (from cypherpunks to open-source movements).
- It raises new questions about how we define identity, ownership, community, and governance in an increasingly digital world.

Next, we will build on this foundation by exploring the core technologies that make Web3 possible, starting with the fundamental innovation: the blockchain.

(Exercises – History & Philosophy:) 1. **Compare Web2 and Web3:** Identify three features of the Web2 internet and describe their Web3 counterparts (e.g. centralized social network vs. decentralized social platform). What advantages does the Web3 version offer, and what challenges might it face? 2. **Decentralization Trade-offs:** Consider a non-digital system (such as a government, or a supply chain). What might be the benefits and drawbacks of decentralizing that system? Relate your answer to blockchain examples (for instance, replacing a central bank with Bitcoin). 3. **Digital Legacy Thought Experiment:** Imagine a future where most of your personal data, achievements, and assets are secured as tokens or entries on a blockchain. How might this change the way you plan your life and legacy? What new ethical or legal questions arise (think about inheritance, privacy after death, etc.)? 4. **Metaverse Governance:** Research how a current blockchain-based metaverse (like Decentraland or The Sandbox) is governed. Does it implement community voting or decentralized decision-making? Analyze it in terms of Hobbes' Leviathan – is there a risk of a centralized power emerging, and how could that be mitigated?

Blockchain Technology: The Backbone of Web3

At the heart of Web3 is the *blockchain* – a novel combination of distributed networking, cryptography, and consensus algorithms. This chapter provides a layered understanding of blockchain technology. We'll start from first principles and build up to the advanced mechanics that make blockchains secure and decentralized. Whether you are new to blockchains or already familiar, this chapter has something for each level of reader, including technical deep-dives and current research frontiers.

Blockchain Fundamentals *(Beginner)*

What is a blockchain? In essence, a blockchain is a **digital ledger** that is duplicated across a network of computers (nodes). Imagine a Google Spreadsheet that's shared with thousands of computers around the world. Everyone can see and add to it, but once entries are added and confirmed, no one can alter previous entries. That append-only ledger, secured by cryptography, is the blockchain.

Key characteristics of blockchains:

- **Decentralized:** No single authority controls the ledger. All participants collectively ensure its integrity.
- **Immutable:** Entries (transactions) once confirmed are extremely difficult to change. This is because they're linked using cryptographic hashes – each block of transactions contains a hash (fingerprint) of the previous block. If someone tries to tamper with an old record, that block's hash changes, breaking the chain and alerting the network.
- **Transparent:** In public blockchains like Bitcoin and Ethereum, all transaction data is visible to everyone (though pseudonymous). This transparency builds trust, since anyone can audit the ledger.

- **Secure by Consensus:** The network uses consensus algorithms to agree on what new transactions to add. In Bitcoin's Proof-of-Work, for example, nodes (miners) compete to solve a cryptographic puzzle; the winner proposes the next block and is rewarded. The puzzle solution is hard to find but easy to verify, making it nearly impossible for a bad actor to forge a valid block without immense computational power.

A useful analogy is a **record book** passed around a crowd:

- Instead of one person writing all entries, everyone takes turns (but only after the crowd agrees they followed the rules).
- Each new page of the book references the content of the previous page (so you can't swap out an old page without everyone noticing).
- Everyone has a copy of the book, so there's no single "true" copy that can be altered in secret.

In practical terms: A blockchain stores **transactions** (e.g., "Alice sends 2 ETH to Bob") in batches called **blocks**, each block referencing the prior one. The first block is the "genesis block." Over time you get a long chain – hence *block-chain*. Because of the linking, the longer the chain, the more secure the history becomes (an attacker would have to redo the work of all subsequent blocks to change a single block deep in the chain).

Tip for beginners: It's okay if this feels abstract. Think of it like a *shared Google Doc ledger* where any change is permanently tracked and locked in, except there's no Google – just the document editing rules enforced by code and agreed upon by all participants.

How Blockchain Transactions Work *(Intermediate)*

Let's go a level deeper and follow a typical transaction lifecycle on a blockchain like Ethereum:

1. **Transaction Creation:** Alice wants to send 2 ETH to Bob. Using her wallet software, she creates a transaction – basically a message saying "Transfer 2 ETH from Alice's account to Bob's account," and she **signs** it with her private key. This digital signature is crucial; it proves the transaction is legitimately from Alice (since only she has her private cryptographic key) and not altered in transit deloitte.com.
2. **Broadcasting:** Alice's signed transaction is broadcast to the Ethereum network. It propagates to many nodes (this is a gossip-like peer-to-peer network).
3. **Mempool:** The transaction enters a "mempool" (memory pool) of pending transactions at each miner/validator node. Think of mempool as a waiting room.
4. **Block Proposal:** A miner (in Proof-of-Work) or validator (in Proof-of-Stake) bundles Alice's transaction with others into a block candidate. In Ethereum's current Proof-of-Stake system, a validator is randomly chosen (weighted by the amount of ETH they staked) to propose the next block at each time slot.
5. **Consensus & Verification:** The proposer/miner must demonstrate the required condition (PoW solution or be the designated PoS proposer). The candidate block is then shared. Other nodes verify that:
    - The transactions are valid (no one is spending more than they have, signatures are correct, etc.).
    - The block follows all rules (correct data format, correct reference to previous block hash, etc.).
6. **Block Finalization:** If the block is valid, it gets appended to the chain. In PoW, once miners accept it and move on to mine the next block, the chain grows. In PoS Ethereum, a block goes through rounds of attestation by committees of validators and is considered *finalized* after a checkpoint passes a supermajority vote (making it extremely difficult to revert).
7. **Transaction Confirmation:** Alice and Bob see that the transaction is included in block X. Bob now effectively has 2 more ETH (and Alice 2 less). Initially, they may wait for a few

more blocks to be mined on top of block X – each additional block is more "confirmation" that the network accepts this transaction as permanent. (On Bitcoin, 6 confirmations ~ around 1 hour, is a common safety standard).
8. **Global Ledger Updated:** Every full node in the network updates its copy of the ledger to reflect the new balances for Alice and Bob.

Cryptographic underpinnings: Blockchain security relies on cryptography:

- **Hash Functions:** A hash function takes input data and produces a fixed-size string (e.g., 256-bit) that looks random. It's one-way: easy to compute, infeasible to reverse. In blockchains, each block contains a hash of the previous block (usually part of the block header). Even a tiny change in a block's data produces a completely different hash, so hashes act as tamper-evident seals deloitte.com.
- **Digital Signatures:** Based on asymmetric cryptography (public/private keys), they allow a user to prove ownership of funds. For example, Bitcoin and Ethereum use ECDSA (Elliptic Curve Digital Signature Algorithm). Quantum computing threatens this, as we'll discuss later, because Shor's algorithm can theoretically derive private keys from public keys given enough quantum power. But for now, classical computers can't break it, so signatures are secure.

Block Structure: A block typically contains:

- A list of transactions (and each transaction might include information like sender, receiver, amount, and other data like smart contract calls).
- A timestamp.
- A reference (hash) to the previous block.
- A **nonce** (in PoW, the number miners adjust to search for a valid hash).

- Other metadata (in Ethereum, for instance, the block header includes the difficulty, gas limit, etc., and in PoS there are different fields like proposer index).

As an intermediate learner, you should understand that a blockchain is essentially an **ordered, cryptographically-linked list of transaction batches**, maintained by a network that follows strict consensus rules. These rules define what makes a block valid and how participants agree on one chain of history. The longest (or heaviest) valid chain is typically considered the truth.

Consensus Algorithms and Security *(Advanced)*

One of the brilliant aspects of blockchain design is how **consensus algorithms** allow a decentralized network to agree on a single version of the truth. Here we outline a few major consensus mechanisms, along with their mathematical or algorithmic underpinnings:

- **Proof of Work (PoW):** Used by Bitcoin, and until recently Ethereum. Here, miners compete to solve a difficult computational puzzle (finding a hash of the block header that is below a target value, which requires trying many nonce values). The probability of mining a block is proportional to one's computational power relative to the network. Security: To attack (e.g., rewrite history), an adversary would need >50% of total mining power to outpace the honest miners – extremely costly in terms of hardware and electricity. The **difficulty** adjusts such that blocks come at a steady rate (e.g., Bitcoin ~10 minutes) even if the total hash power changes. A simplified model: if p is the probability a given nonce yields a valid hash, miners perform a Bernoulli trial each hash. The expected number of hashes to find a valid block is $1/p$. The target value in Bitcoin adjusts to keep $1/p$ such that on average one block/10 minutes is found given the current global hash rate.

- **Proof of Stake (PoS):** Used by modern Ethereum (as of 2022) and others like Cardano, Tezos. Here, the chance to propose or validate a block is proportional to the amount of cryptocurrency one locks up (stakes) in the system. Instead of expending energy, validators put their funds at risk: if they act dishonestly (e.g., validate conflicting histories), they can be *slashed* (losing some or all of their stake). PoS involves random selection algorithms and often BFT (Byzantine Fault Tolerant) consensus protocols among validators. For example, Ethereum's consensus (the Casper-FFG combined with LMD-Ghost rules) ensures finality by requiring 2/3 of validators (by stake weight) to sign onto checkpoints; if they tried to finalize two conflicting histories, they'd be mathematically caught and penalized. The security of PoS is analyzed under game theory – honest majority (by stake) is assumed. An attack would require an adversary to control >2/3 of the stake (for finalization attacks) or >50% for liveness/equivocation attacks, which means buying up a huge fraction of the currency (making it economically self-defeating in many ways).
- **Other Algorithms:** There are many variants/alternatives:
    - *Delegated Proof of Stake (DPoS):* used by EOS, TRON, etc., where token holders vote in a fixed number of "delegates" who produce blocks in round-robin. It's fast but more semi-decentralized (consensus in the hands of 21–100 nodes typically).
    - *Practical Byzantine Fault Tolerance (PBFT):* a classical consensus algorithm for a fixed set of validators, achieving finality in a single round of voting. Used in permissioned (private) blockchains and as components in hybrids.
    - *Proof of Authority:* where a known set of validators take turns (useful in testnets or consortium chains).
    - *Nakamoto Consensus vs. BFT:* It's worth noting Bitcoin's PoW is an *open, probabilistic consensus* (forks can happen, and longest chain eventually "wins" probabilistically), whereas many newer chains

aim for *fast finality* (once a block is finalized, it's final). This often involves multi-round voting by validators (introducing a notion of time slots or epochs).

Mathematical Rigor: Blockchain protocols are often analyzed in terms of *probability* and *cryptographic hardness*:

- For PoW, one can calculate the probability of a fork: e.g., the chance two miners find a block at the same time, or an attacker with fraction f of hash power to ever catch up after being k blocks behind (this drops exponentially with k).
- For cryptography, hardness assumptions (like SHA-256 is collision-resistant; ECDSA is unforgeable under chosen message attack) are the foundation. Formal proofs exist that if these assumptions hold and if >50% of mining power is honest, Bitcoin's blockchain will remain secure (with probability overwhelming in k, where k confirmations reduce risk).
- In PoS and BFT consensus, proof techniques involve showing no conflicting blocks can both reach finality, using *safety* proofs (invariant: two-thirds of honest weighted votes cannot sign two different histories) and *liveness* proofs (the protocol eventually confirms new transactions if less than one-third are adversarial and network conditions are decent).

Scalability and the Trilemma: Advanced readers will know that one of blockchain's big challenges is scaling up throughput without sacrificing security or decentralization – this is often framed as the *Blockchain Trilemma*. Projects are exploring:

- *Layer 2 solutions:* like the Lightning Network (Bitcoin) or rollups (Ethereum) that process many transactions off-chain and settle the result on chain.
- *Sharding:* Ethereum's roadmap includes sharding to split the network into multiple chains that run in parallel, increasing capacity.

- *Alternative architectures:* DAG-based ledgers (like IOTA's Tangle or Fantom's Opera) or newer consensus like Avalanche protocol that uses random sampling for consensus.

Current research is vibrant: everything from **zero-knowledge proofs** (e.g., zkSNARKs) to compress history or allow private transactions, to **post-quantum cryptography** to upgrade signature schemes before quantum computers arrive, is being examined.

(Exercises – Blockchain Tech): 1. **Immutability in Action:** Suppose an attacker controls 30% of Bitcoin's mining power. Explain why they cannot change a transaction from 10 blocks ago without also re-mining those 10 blocks. Calculate the probability that this attacker could catch up if honest miners have a 7-block lead (hint: use a simplified model or reasoning). 2. **Consensus Compare:** List the pros and cons of Proof-of-Work vs Proof-of-Stake in terms of security, energy use, centralization risk, and attack scenarios. 3. **Design a Blockchain:** If you were designing a blockchain for a permissioned consortium of 20 banks, which consensus mechanism might you choose and why? How would it differ from Bitcoin's approach? 4. **Scaling Debate:** Research Ethereum's proposed sharding or a Layer 2 like Optimistic Rollups. Describe in your own words how it improves throughput. What are the new complexities or trust assumptions (if any) that it introduces? 5. **Cryptography Task:** (a) Take a simple hash function analog (for exercise): convert an input number to its square mod 100 (this is not secure, just an illustration). If your "block" data is number 7, and previous block's "hash" was 16, create a new block hash as hash(7 || 16) i.e. concatenation. (b) Explain how a real hash like SHA-256 being collision-resistant helps prevent two different sequences of transactions from producing the same block hash (why is that important?).

Smart Contracts and Decentralized Applications (dApps)

With the blockchain fundamentals in hand, we turn to *smart contracts* – self-executing programs stored on the blockchain – and the decentralized applications that are built from them. Smart contracts are what make blockchains like Ethereum so powerful, enabling complex transactions and automation beyond simple send/receive of cryptocurrency. This chapter will explore smart contract concepts from simple to advanced, including how they are written, executed, secured, and used to create full-fledged dApps.

Introduction to Smart Contracts *(Beginner)*

What is a smart contract? A smart contract is like a small computer program that lives on the blockchain. It has code (functions) and data (state), and it runs exactly as programmed without downtime, censorship, or third-party interference docs.soliditylang.org. The term *contract* is used because they often handle agreements – for example, a simple smart contract might say "if person A sends 1 Ether to this contract, then release a digital asset to person A" – analogous to a vending machine. Nick Szabo, who coined the term in the 1990s, gave the vending machine as an analogy: you drop a coin, you either get your snack or your coin back – and the mechanism enforces that without needing a shopkeeper. Smart contracts bring that automation to digital agreements.

How they work on a blockchain: Taking Ethereum as the archetype:

- Ethereum has a **virtual machine** (EVM – Ethereum Virtual Machine) that can execute code written in its instruction set (bytecode). Developers write smart contracts in high-level languages (like Solidity or Vyper for Ethereum), which compile down to EVM bytecode.
- When you deploy a smart contract, you are actually creating a special transaction that contains the contract's bytecode. The network miners/validators process that transaction,

which results in a new contract account on the blockchain with the code stored at that address.
- From then on, anyone can interact with the contract by sending transactions to its address, calling its functions. The code executes on every node (ensuring consensus on the outcome), and can read/write its internal storage or even call other contracts.

Key properties:

- Smart contract code is **immutable** once deployed (in most cases). If a bug is found, you can't patch it like regular software – you'd have to deploy a new contract. Some contracts are upgradeable via proxy patterns, but that requires forethought in design.
- They hold and manage assets: A contract can hold native cryptocurrency (like ETH) and keep track of tokens (like an ERC-20 token ledger) in its storage variables.
- **Deterministic execution:** Given the same state and input, a contract's code will produce the same output on all nodes. This is critical so the whole network stays in sync. It also means contract languages avoid non-deterministic actions (like no network calls to random APIs – everything must be within the blockchain environment).

Example: A simple example is an ERC-20 token contract (a standard for fungible tokens on Ethereum). The contract keeps a ledger mapping addresses to balances, and has functions `transfer(address to, uint amount)` which moves tokens by updating balances (provided the sender has enough), and `balanceOf(address)` to view balances. This contract effectively **acts as a bank** for that token, but with the rules hard-coded and transparently visible. No one can arbitrarily change the balances; only the programmed rules (transfers, minting if allowed, etc.) can change the state. This concept underpins a lot of DeFi (Decentralized Finance) – instead of a bank or exchange keeping the ledger of who owns what, a smart contract does it in a transparent, open way.

As a beginner, understand that smart contracts enable *trustless cooperation*. People or systems can make agreements ("I'll pay X for Y asset", "I'll lend you money if you put collateral") without needing a centralized intermediary, because the contract enforces the terms. If conditions aren't met, the contract can automatically revert the transaction or impose penalties. Everything runs on the blockchain, gaining the same security (tamper-proof, always available).

Building and Deploying Contracts *(Intermediate)*

In practice, how do you write and deploy a smart contract? Let's go through a simple development scenario:

Writing the Contract: Suppose we want to create a simple **Crowdfunding** contract. We decide on parameters: the fundraising goal, a deadline, and functions for contributors to send funds and for the initiator to withdraw if the goal is met. We write this in Solidity. For example:

solidity
CopyEdit
```
// SPDX-License-Identifier: MIT
pragma solidity ^0.8.0;
contract CrowdFund {
    address public owner;
    uint public goal;
    uint public deadline;
    mapping(address => uint) public contributions;
    bool public goalReached;

    constructor(uint _goal, uint _duration) {
        owner = msg.sender;
```

```solidity
        goal = _goal;
        deadline = block.timestamp + _duration;
    }
    function contribute() public payable {
        require(block.timestamp < deadline, "Fundraising ended");
        contributions[msg.sender] += msg.value;
    }
    function withdraw() public {
        require(block.timestamp >= deadline, "Too early");
        if(address(this).balance >= goal) {
            // Goal reached
            require(msg.sender == owner, "Only owner withdraws");
            goalReached = true;
            payable(owner).transfer(address(this).balance);
        } else {
            // Goal not reached: contributors can get refund
            uint amount = contributions[msg.sender];
            contributions[msg.sender] = 0;
            payable(msg.sender).transfer(amount);
        }
    }
}
```

1. This is a simplified example. It shows a contract storing data (owner, goal, etc.), receiving funds (the `contribute()` function is marked `payable` to accept ETH), and logic to withdraw either to the project owner if success or refunds to

contributors if not. Each contributor's amount is tracked in a mapping.
2. **Testing Locally:** Developers usually test contracts in local or testnet environments. Tools like **Remix (web IDE)** or frameworks like **Truffle** or **Hardhat** help in compiling and running tests. For instance, we'd test that before the deadline contributions accumulate, after deadline if balance < goal contributors can get refunds, etc.
3. **Deploying:** To deploy on a real network (Ethereum mainnet or a testnet like Goerli), you use a wallet or script to send a deployment transaction. This transaction's `to` field is empty (meaning it's a contract creation) and `data` field has the compiled bytecode + constructor arguments. You also must pay gas (the fee for computation and storage on Ethereum). The network miners/validators execute the constructor code and if successful, assign an address to the new contract. From then, the contract code is immutable at that address.
4. **Interacting with Contracts:** Users interact by sending transactions calling functions. If a function is marked `view` or `pure` (read-only), it doesn't cost gas if called off-chain (just reading state doesn't require a transaction, one can query a node for the data). But any state-changing function (like our `contribute` or `withdraw`) requires a transaction and gas. Tools like **web3.js** or **ethers.js** in a dApp's frontend allow integration: e.g., a web interface that calls `contract.methods.contribute().send({from: user, value: amount})` when a user clicks a contribute button, using their Web3 wallet (like MetaMask) to sign the transaction.
5. **dApps:** A decentralized application might be composed of:
    - Smart contracts (back-end logic on blockchain).
    - A front-end (web or mobile) that interacts with those contracts (via wallet).
    - Sometimes off-chain or decentralized storage for large data (e.g., IPFS or Arweave if the app needs to store files). The key is the core logic (who can do

what, when) is enforced by smart contracts on-chain, giving users guarantees not present in traditional apps.

Gas and Efficiency: Each operation in a smart contract consumes *gas* (a unit measuring computation or storage usage). The sender of a transaction pays for gas in ETH (or the chain's native token). Complex loops or heavy storage writes can be expensive. This is why smart contract developers must consider efficiency. For instance, writing to Ethereum's storage is far costlier than reading it, and loops over large arrays can hit gas limits. In our CrowdFund example, notice we didn't provide a function to list all contributors — because storing a dynamic list or iterating might be impractical. Instead, contributors individually withdraw their funds; it's a pattern pushing some complexity to the users to keep the contract simple (common in solidity to avoid loops that could run out of gas).

Standards and Interoperability: The community has developed standards (protocols) that contracts often follow so they can interoperate:

- **ERC-20:** Standard interface for fungible tokens (defines functions like `totalSupply()`, `transfer()`, etc.). This way, wallets and exchanges can support any token that implements ERC-20.
- **ERC-721:** Standard for NFTs (non-fungible tokens).
- **ERC-1155:** Multi-token standard (fungible and non-fungible in one contract).
- Many others (for decentralized identity, governance, etc.).

Following standards is crucial so your contract can plug into the existing Web3 ecosystem (for example, an ERC-20 token contract will automatically be usable by DeFi protocols like Uniswap for trading or Compound for lending, since those protocols expect standard functions).

Smart Contract Security and Best Practices *(Advanced)*

Smart contracts, once deployed, manage real assets and cannot be easily changed. This makes security **paramount**. There have been notable hacks and bugs (like the infamous DAO hack in 2016 articlegateway.com, which exploited a reentrancy bug to steal ~$50M in ETH, or more recent DeFi hacks leaking hundreds of millions). Here we discuss common security considerations and the mathematical rigor behind them:

- **Formal Verification:** This is the process of using mathematical methods to prove the correctness of a program relative to a specification. Some contracts (especially in high-stakes scenarios) have been formally verified. For instance, makerDAO's Multi-Collateral DAI contract was written in a subset of Python and formally verified to ensure that under certain conditions it maintained collateralization. Formal methods involve creating a model of the contract and using solvers or proof assistants to check properties (like "no funds can be lost or locked up forever unless explicitly allowed"). Tools like Coq, Isabelle, or even domain-specific languages (like K or Dafny for Ethereum) can be used. However, this is complex and not yet widespread for all contracts.
- **Common Vulnerabilities:**
    - *Reentrancy:* If a contract calls an external contract, that external contract might call back into the original function before the first invocation finished, messing up assumptions. The remedy is often to use the "Checks-Effects-Interactions" pattern: update state (effects) **before** calling external contracts, so that if they reenter, the state already reflects the deduction. For example, in our `withdraw()` above, when refunding, we set `contributions[msg.sender]`

= 0 before transferring funds out, to prevent reentrant calls withdrawing multiple times.
  - *Integer Overflow/Underflow:* Earlier Solidity versions needed care with arithmetic (now with Solidity 0.8+, arithmetic throws on overflow by default which is safer). If not handled, an overflow could cause logic issues (like if a token's balance overflowed to zero).
  - *Access Control:* Many bugs are simply forgetting to restrict functions that should only be called by specific people (e.g., an `init()` function that could be called by anyone not just the owner).
  - *Randomness:* Blockchain is a deterministic environment, so getting a secure random number is tricky. Using something like `block.timestamp` or `blockhash` for randomness can be manipulated by miners. Advanced methods use oracles or commit-reveal schemes or verifiable random functions (VRFs).
  - *Denial of Service (DoS):* For instance, if a contract's logic processes an array of users and one user can make their entry extremely large (or gas-costly) to process, it might block others from being handled in the same block. Another DoS vector is failing to handle when a contract (address) receiving Ether via `transfer` reverts – in the DAO hack aftermath, the shift to using `send` or `call` with limited gas and checking return values became best practice.
  - *Flash Loan attacks:* Unique to DeFi context, but since someone can borrow huge funds with no collateral briefly (as long as they return in the same transaction), contracts that assume nobody can have more than X assets at a time or manipulate prices within one transaction have been exploited. This is more of an economic exploit than a bug in code.
- **Auditing and Tools:** Professional audits are a norm for serious projects – experts review code line by line. Tools like

static analyzers (MythX, Slither) can catch some issues automatically. The ecosystem has learned a lot from past failures, and resources like the **SWC (Smart Contract Weakness Classification)** registry enumerate known issues.

Algorithmic aspects: The EVM is a stack-based architecture, Turing-complete but gas-limited. Advanced developers sometimes reason in opcodes and gas costs (for example, the `SSTORE` operation (storing a 32-byte word) costs 20,000 gas when setting a non-zero to zero or vice versa, etc.). An interesting rigorous result: Ethereum's gas mechanism is designed to make any infinite loop or excessive computation financially unviable (the Halting problem can't be solved generally, but at least you'll run out of gas and the transaction will revert if you try something crazy).

Upgradability: Because smart contracts are immutable, a pattern emerged: **proxy contracts**. In this pattern, users interact with a proxy contract that delegates every call to a logic contract (address of which is stored in proxy's storage). By updating that address (only allowed to an admin), you can upgrade the logic. This introduces complexity and some risk (and trust in the admin), but is used by many projects to allow iteration. If you see a contract address like a major stablecoin (USDC), often it's a proxy pointing to an upgradable logic contract.

Real-world example for context: The Ethereum *DAO hack (2016)* exploited a reentrancy bug in a crowdfunding-like contract (The DAO was a decentralized venture fund). The attacker repeatedly siphoned funds by calling the withdraw function recursively before the contract could update its balance, draining a huge amount articlegateway.com. This led to Ethereum's controversial fork to restore the funds (and the creation of Ethereum Classic for those who opposed the fork). Post-DAO, the ecosystem strongly emphasized secure patterns: always update state before transferring Ether out, and consider using **ReentrancyGuard** (a simple mutex-like contract that prevents reentrant calls) in functions that send Ether.

As an advanced reader, you should be aware that writing safe smart contracts often requires adversarial thinking. Unlike traditional apps, you can't rely on obscurity (code is public) or quick patches. The code *is* the law (in Ethereum's case, *"code is law"* became a mantra). Thus, rigorous testing and sometimes even mathematical proofs are utilized to ensure contracts do exactly what is intended and nothing more.

(Exercises – Smart Contracts): *1.* **Write a Simple Contract:** Write pseudocode or actual Solidity for a simple **escrow** contract: Party A deposits funds that Party B can withdraw only if A (or perhaps a trusted arbitrator) gives a signal, otherwise A can reclaim after a deadline. Think about what state variables and functions you need. *2.* **Identify the Bug:** The following Solidity function is intended to allow a user to withdraw their balance: `function withdrawBalance() public { require(balances[msg.sender] > 0); msg.sender.call{value: balances[msg.sender]}(""); balances[msg.sender] = 0; }`. What potential vulnerability exists here? How would you fix it? *3.* **Gas Calculation:** If a user calls a function that executes a loop iterating over an array of 5 items and inside the loop it does a simple arithmetic operation and a storage write for each item, roughly estimate the gas cost (assume ~20k per storage write, ~5 gas per arithmetic op, ~50 gas loop overhead per iteration, plus base ~21k gas per transaction). This is just to get a feel for costs. What if the array had 500 items? *4.* **Smart Contract Ethics:** Consider the immutability of smart contracts: if a bug causes loss of funds for users, do you think blockchain platforms should ever intervene (as happened in The DAO fork)? Debate the pros and cons of the "code is law" principle in such scenarios. *5.* **ERC-20 Standard Reading:** Look up the ERC-20 standard. Why do you think functions like `approve`/`transferFrom` exist in addition to `transfer`? (Hint:

think about allowing a smart contract to spend tokens on your behalf, e.g. a decentralized exchange.) How does this pattern compare to how bank accounts or credit cards work in traditional finance?

Decentralized Finance (DeFi) and Hybrid Finance

One of the most impactful applications of Web3 has been **Decentralized Finance (DeFi)** – an ecosystem of financial applications built on blockchain networks. DeFi enables services like lending, borrowing, trading, insurance, and more, without traditional intermediaries like banks or brokers. This chapter explores the components of DeFi, the protocols that make it work, and the emerging concept of **Hybrid Finance (HyFi)** which bridges DeFi with traditional finance. We'll look at case studies of DeFi projects and dive into some quantitative models underlying them.

DeFi Essentials: Financial Services without Intermediaries *(Beginner)*

Imagine replicating the services of a bank or an investment broker using only code on the blockchain:

- **Cryptocurrency Exchanges:** Instead of a centralized exchange (like Coinbase) holding order books and custody of assets, DeFi uses **Automated Market Makers (AMMs)** like Uniswap where liquidity pools allow users to swap tokens directly from their wallets.
- **Lending and Borrowing:** Platforms like Compound or Aave let users lend out their crypto and earn interest, or borrow by providing collateral – all managed by smart contracts. There's no banker in the middle; interest rates float based on supply and demand coded into the protocol.
- **Stablecoins:** Cryptocurrencies pegged to stable assets (like USD) provide a stable unit of account in DeFi. Some are

backed by reserves (USDC, USDT), others are algorithmic or over-collateralized on-chain (DAI from MakerDAO, which is generated by locking ETH and other assets in vaults).
- **Derivatives and Assets:** DeFi also offers synthetic assets, futures, options, etc., via protocols like Synthetix or dYdX.
- **Payments and Money Transfers:** While basic cryptocurrency transactions cover this, DeFi extends it with programmable features (like streaming payments by the second via Sablier, or automated escrow via smart contracts).
- **Insurance:** Decentralized insurance like Nexus Mutual provides coverage for smart contract failures, governed by members who stake and vote on claims.

The core idea is **disintermediation**: removing middlemen. Users interact with smart contracts directly:

- If you trade on Uniswap, you are effectively invoking a function on a liquidity pool contract that swaps tokens according to its algorithm.
- When you deposit funds into Compound, a smart contract credits you interest-bearing cTokens and makes your liquidity available to borrowers.

For a beginner, DeFi can be thought of as **"Money Legos"** – different financial contracts that can stack/combine because they share the blockchain as a common settlement layer. For instance, you could take a DAI loan from MakerDAO, swap it for ETH on Uniswap, and put that ETH into Compound to earn interest – all these pieces are interoperable because they use standard tokens and contracts on Ethereum.

User experience: Typically, users need a Web3 wallet (like MetaMask) loaded with some crypto (for gas fees and assets to interact with). They then visit a dApp's website, which connects to their wallet, and they can initiate transactions (e.g., click "Deposit" in a lending app). The transaction goes to the blockchain and, once confirmed, the action is done trustlessly.

While the idea is revolutionary, it's important to note to beginners that DeFi comes with risks: smart contract bugs, volatile asset prices, and no FDIC insurance or chargebacks if something goes wrong. We'll discuss risks in advanced sections.

How DeFi Protocols Work: AMMs, Lending Pools, and More *(Intermediate)*

This section takes a closer look at the mechanisms behind popular DeFi protocols, including some math that governs them.

Automated Market Makers (AMMs): Traditional exchanges use order books (buyers and sellers place orders). AMMs replace this with pools of tokens. For example, a Uniswap pool for ETH/USDC holds some amount of ETH and some amount of USDC provided by liquidity providers. The pool quotes a price automatically based on a formula. The most common formula is the **constant product formula**: $x * y = k$ acala.network. Here x = quantity of token A, y = quantity of token B in the pool, and k is constant (ignoring fees) during trades. If someone swaps token A for B, they add A to the pool and remove B until the product $x*y$ returns to the same k. This formula results in a **price curve**: price of token A in terms of B is determined by the ratio y/x (the derivative of the product invariant).

For instance, if a pool has 100 ETH and 200,000 USDC, the implied price of 1 ETH is 2000 USDC (because removing a tiny amount Δx of ETH yields Δy of USDC such that $(100+\Delta x)*(200000-\Delta y)$=constant, leading roughly to $\Delta y/\Delta x = 2000$ near equilibrium).

AMMs are elegant because anyone can trade against them at any time, but there are trade-offs:

- Liquidity providers suffer **impermanent loss** – if prices diverge, the value of their pooled assets is less than if they simply held them, due to the product formula. However, they earn trading fees which can compensate if volume is high.
- Slippage: The more you trade at once, the more you move the price (since k is constant, large trades significantly change x and y). This is why large trades can incur slippage in price.

Despite simplicity, AMMs unlocked huge activity because they removed the need for active market makers and order book infrastructure on-chain. The constant product AMM (Uniswap's model) is most famous, but others exist (Balancer uses a generalized mean for >2 tokens pools, Curve's stablecoin AMM uses a formula optimized for assets that trade near parity, etc.).

Lending Pools (Compound/Aave model): These protocols create pooled funds for each asset. For example, Compound's ETH pool might have 50,000 ETH supplied by lenders. Borrowers can take ETH from this pool if they provide sufficient collateral in another asset (say, they lock 150% worth in DAI to borrow ETH). Interest rates are set algorithmically: when a pool is highly utilized (many borrows relative to supply), the interest rate spikes up to attract more suppliers and deter borrowing; when there's plenty of liquidity, rates are lower. Typically, a utilization-based model is used: e.g., interest rate = 2% + (Utilization * 20%), and perhaps a jump after a threshold. If a borrower's collateral falls below required ratios due to price changes or borrowing more, anyone can liquidate their position: the smart contract allows liquidators to repay the borrower's debt and take a chunk of their collateral at a slight discount (incentivizing keeping the system solvent). This mechanism has a clear algorithmic aspect: it's effectively a continuous margin requirement enforced by code.

Stablecoins: To maintain a peg, different designs:

- Asset-backed: USDC is simple – 1 USDC is backed by $1 in a bank. Here trust in a centralized issuer (Circle) is the mechanism.
- Crypto-collateralized: DAI is generated by collateral (like ETH) locked at typically 150% or more. If ETH's price drops too much, the system sells the collateral via auctions to keep DAI fully backed. There's a stability fee (interest) and other parameters, tuned via governance (MakerDAO token holders vote). The economics can be complex: they recently added a Dai Savings Rate and have income from collateral vaults, so you can analyze Maker as a decentralized central bank with balance sheet and monetary policy (targeting 1 DAI = $1).
- Algorithmic (uncollateralized or partially): e.g., older ones like Ampleforth (rebases supply) or TerraUSD (before its collapse) tried to maintain value via algorithms and market incentives. Many algorithmic stablecoins have struggled or failed because keeping a peg purely via arbitrage incentives in volatile markets is very challenging.

Yield Farming and Liquidity Mining: These terms refer to protocols distributing tokens to users as incentives for providing liquidity or using the platform. For example, Compound famously started *liquidity mining* by giving COMP governance tokens to borrowers and lenders, effectively subsidizing use. Yield farmers would hop around protocols chasing the highest APY (annual percentage yield), often stacking yields (e.g., providing liquidity on Uniswap and then staking the liquidity token somewhere else to earn another token reward). This led to the "DeFi Summer" of 2020 with explosive growth. While not a single protocol mechanism, yield farming has a game-theoretic angle: it bootstraps network effects but can also cause mercenary behavior where liquidity is not "sticky" once rewards dry up.

Decentralized Autonomous Organizations (DAOs) in DeFi: Most DeFi protocols have governance tokens (COMP for Compound, AAVE for Aave, UNI for Uniswap, etc.) which allow holders to vote on parameters and upgrades. These token votes effectively control the protocol, making major DeFi platforms into DAOs. Governance may decide interest rate formulas, collateral lists, fee parameters, or even smart contract upgrades. This is decentralization in action, though voter participation and power distributions vary (often big investors or the team hold significant governance power early on).

Mathematical Models in DeFi: A few examples:

- *Bonding curves:* The AMM pricing is one example. Also used in token sale mechanisms or automated continuous token models.
- *Interest rate curves:* Modeled as piecewise linear or exponential based on utilization.
- *Risk models:* Value-at-Risk for liquidity providers, or solvency probability for lending pools given volatility. Some research applies traditional finance models (like Black-Scholes for options in DeFi context, or Monte Carlo simulations for liquidation risk).
- *Game theory:* Analyzing equilibrium when multiple parties interact – e.g., will users behave honestly in a protocol, will arbitrage traders keep prices aligned between DEXs and CEXs (central exchanges)? Usually yes, arbitrage is a key piece (it's what keeps Uniswap prices roughly in line with external markets: if ETH is cheaper on Uniswap than Binance, arbitragers will buy on Uniswap and sell on Binance until prices align, and in doing so, they push Uniswap's price back up by removing ETH from the pool).

A concrete case study in DeFi could be **MakerDAO and Hybrid Finance** which we'll dedicate a section to below, as it transitions into Hybrid Finance.

(At this intermediate level, consider exploring one specific DeFi protocol's documentation for deeper understanding – e.g., the Compound Whitepaper or Uniswap's whitepaper which derives the constant product formula and liquidity provider returns.)

Advanced DeFi: Algorithmic Mechanisms and Risks (Advanced)

For those with a strong grasp of DeFi basics, let's discuss some advanced topics:

- **Impermanent Loss Math:** For an AMM, if the price of token A increases relative to B, liquidity providers end up holding less of token A (more of token B) than initially. The impermanent loss (IL) formula (for constant product AMM) for a price move of ratio r is: $IL = 1 - ((2*sqrt(r)) / (r+1))$. For example, if price doubles (r=2), IL ≈ 5.7%. If price halves (r=0.5, which is r=2 in opposite direction), same 5.7%. Large moves (r>>1 or <<1) yield IL approaching significant % (for r=5, IL ~ 25.5%). This is called "impermanent" because if prices return to the initial state, the loss reverses. LPs must weigh trading fee earnings versus IL.
- **AMM arbitrage and efficiency:** Each block, arbitragers ensure AMM pools reflect external prices by profiting from discrepancies. There's a whole field of *DEX arbitrage optimization*; in fact, arbitrage bots (often using Flashbots or private transaction flow to execute) compete for these profits, which is an example of *Miner Extractable Value (MEV)* – the value that miners/validators (or generally the block proposer) can extract by ordering transactions in certain ways. MEV has become a significant topic: too much MEV can lead to front-running and user losses, so now protocols like Flashbots are mitigating it by providing auctions for ordering.
- **Collateral and Liquidation Modeling:** In lending, determining safe collateral factors requires analyzing volatility and liquidity of assets. E.g., if you allow a new token as collateral, you'd set a conservative collateral factor

(maybe 50%, meaning you can borrow up to half the value) if it's volatile or illiquid. Advanced models use historical simulation or stress tests to decide these. When markets crash, liquidators step in – an ideal design ensures the incentives are enough so loans get liquidated *before* they become undercollateralized. If not, the protocol could have bad debt (borrowers owing more than their collateral covers). For example, in MakerDAO, if auctions don't cover the shortfall, they have a mechanism to socialize loss by diluting MKR governance tokens – effectively a lender-of-last-resort concept. This happened in March 2020 "Black Thursday" when a sudden ETH drop and network congestion led to some vaults not getting properly liquidated, and Maker minted extra MKR to cover the losses.

- **Cross-Chain DeFi and Bridges:** Many DeFi activities now span multiple chains (Ethereum, Binance Smart Chain, Solana, Layer2s like Arbitrum, etc.). Bridges allow movement of assets between chains, but they often introduce centralized or new trust assumptions (and have been points of massive hacks themselves). An advanced discussion includes security models of cross-chain bridges and the potential future of inter-chain interoperability (e.g., Cosmos with IBC, Polkadot's cross-parachain messaging).

- **Regulatory arbitrage vs. compliance:** On the socio-technical side, DeFi has drawn regulators' attention (because essentially it can mimic banks/exchanges without KYC). Advanced readers might explore how protocols are decentralizing governance to be more censorship-resistant, or conversely how some DeFi projects are introducing compliance (Aave Arc creating permissioned pools for institutions, for example).

- **Hybrid Smart Contracts:** Chainlink and others talk about "hybrid smart contracts" meaning on-chain code combined with off-chain data/compute via oracles. Price oracles are critical in DeFi (for lending collateral values, etc.) – understanding their design (decentralized networks of reporters, economic incentives, fallback mechanisms) is key at an advanced level. A failure of an oracle can be catastrophic (feeding a wrong price could cause wrongful liquidations or exploitation).

Quantitative Example – Uniswap Trading: Let's say a trader wants to swap 10 ETH for USDC on an ETH/USDC pool with 1000 ETH and 2,000,000 USDC. Constant k = 1000*2,000,000 = 2e9. After adding 10 ETH (assuming small enough not to move price drastically), the new ETH amount is 1010, so the new USDC amount must satisfy 1010 * new_USDC = 2e9, giving new_USDC ≈ 1,980,198. So the trader gets 2,000,000 - 1,980,198 = 19,802 USDC for 10 ETH, implying a price of 1,980.2 USDC/ETH – slightly less than initial 2000 due to slippage. The larger the trade relative to pool size, the worse the slippage (non-linearly so, because of the hyperbolic curve). This example can lead to exercises or formula derivations of trading impact.

Hybrid Finance (HyFi): This term refers to blending DeFi with traditional finance – recognizing that for many real-world uses, completely on-chain isolated systems might not suffice. One early example is the partnership between fintech **Current** (a banking app) and the Polkadot-based DeFi platform **Acala** to create Hybrid Finance services current.com This partnership aimed to connect Current's millions of users (who deal in fiat USD) with DeFi yields and services on Acala, via a seamless interface. The first-of-its-kind integration established a new category of HyFi that *"combines both traditional and decentralized financial applications"*.

Why is HyFi significant? It could:

- Bring more stability and liquidity to DeFi by involving institutional or retail fiat flows.
- Require solving compliance and identity: e.g., KYC'ed users but interacting with smart contracts.
- Potentially dilute some decentralization if not done carefully (if a centralized app is the gatekeeper).
- But it offers a path to mainstream adoption by hiding blockchain complexity behind familiar fintech experiences.

Dr. Justin Goldston and colleagues studied HyFi in *"Decentralized finance (DeFi) to hybrid finance (HyFi) through blockchain: a case-study of Acala and Current"*, highlighting this partnership as a key example en.wikipedia.org. HyFi envisions that instead of viewing traditional finance (TradFi) and DeFi as rivals, they can be integrated: for instance, a regular savings account that actually deposits your money into a DeFi lending protocol behind the scenes for higher yield, or a credit card that lets you spend directly from your crypto holdings while conforming to payment network rules.

The case-study likely concluded that **collaboration** (banks leveraging blockchain for back-end, and DeFi platforms gaining users through banks) could be a more sustainable model than pure competition. It's a reminder that real-world finance and Web3 need not be entirely separate domains; hybrid approaches might shape the next chapter of financial innovation.

(Exercises – DeFi): 1. **AMM Math:** If a Uniswap pool has 500 DAI and 500 USDC (two stablecoins ideally 1:1 value), and someone swaps 100 DAI for USDC, how many USDC do they get (ignore fees)? What is the new price implied by the pool for DAI? (Use x*y=k with x=DAI, y=USDC). 2. **Lending Scenario:** Alice deposits 2 ETH into Compound (assume ETH price $1500, so $3000 value) and borrows 1800 DAI. If the collateral factor for ETH is 75%, is she within the limit? If ETH's price drops 40%, what happens? Show the calculations of her collateral value vs. borrowed value before and after the drop. 3. **Risk Assessment:** Choose a DeFi protocol and identify one technical risk and one economic risk it faces. For

example, Uniswap's technical risk (smart contract bug), economic risk (impermanent loss discouraging LPs if fees are low). Or MakerDAO's technical risk (oracle failure), economic risk (collateral crash). How does the protocol mitigate these risks, if at all? 4. **Hybrid Finance Discussion:** Consider the Current–Acala HyFi partnership. Why might a fintech app want to integrate DeFi yields? What challenges must be overcome (regulatory compliance, user education, technical reliability)? Do you think most users need to know there's blockchain under the hood? 5. **Build a DeFi Portfolio (thought experiment):** If you had $10,000 to allocate in DeFi for a year, how would you distribute it among various opportunities (e.g., provide liquidity on a DEX, lend on Compound, hold some in a volatile asset, etc.) and why? What risks would you be most concerned about (smart contract risk, market risk, etc.) and how would you mitigate them (diversification, insurance, using only audited protocols, etc.)?

Decentralized Autonomous Organizations (DAOs) and Governance

Web3 isn't just about technology – it's about **community governance** enabled by that technology. Decentralized Autonomous Organizations (DAOs) are member-owned communities without centralized leadership, coordinating through token-weighted voting and smart contracts. This chapter examines how DAOs work, the theories of governance behind them, and practical guidance for building and participating in DAOs.

DAO Basics: Communities on the Blockchain (Beginner)

A **Decentralized Autonomous Organization (DAO)** is essentially an organization represented by rules encoded as a computer program (smart contracts), which is controlled by its members and not influenced by a central authority. Imagine an online co-op or club with a shared treasury and decision-making process all handled on-chain.

Key features of a DAO:

- **Decentralized Ownership:** Typically, ownership or membership is represented by tokens. For example, holding 1% of a DAO's governance tokens usually gives you 1% of the voting power. Some DAOs use NFT membership tokens or simply wallet whitelists, but token ownership is common.
- **Autonomous Execution:** The DAO's rules (how proposals are made, how votes are tallied, what threshold passes, what actions can be taken) are enforced by smart contracts. If a vote passes to spend 100 ETH from the treasury on a project, the smart contract can execute that without needing a human intermediary.
- **Transparent and Open:** DAO discussions often happen in the open (forums, Discord, on-chain voting records). The treasury and all votes are visible on the blockchain. Members can come and go (in open DAOs) simply by buying or selling tokens or otherwise obtaining membership.

Examples:

- *The DAO (2016):* The first big DAO was literally called "The DAO" – a venture fund on Ethereum (which got hacked, as discussed earlier). It taught many lessons, and since then DAO frameworks have improved.
- *Protocol DAOs:* Many DeFi projects turn into DAOs by issuing governance tokens (e.g., Uniswap's UNI token holders vote on fee changes or grants). These are essentially DAOs governing a specific protocol.
- *Social DAOs:* Groups like Friends With Benefits (FWB) require holding a certain number of tokens to join an exclusive social club with events and content.
- *Collector DAOs:* PleasrDAO pools funds to acquire high-value NFTs or other collectibles as a group.

- *Grant DAOs:* MetaCartel and others pool funds to issue grants to Web3 projects.
- *Service DAOs:* Decentralized freelance collectives like DXdao or Raid Guild that build and maintain projects, where the DAO structure coordinates the work and payments.

How do members make decisions? Typically through proposals:

1. A member or group submits a proposal (perhaps via a governance interface like Snapshot or on-chain directly). The proposal could be "Allocate 10 ETH to fund Alice's development of feature X" or "Change parameter Y from 5% to 6%" or "Hire person Z for role Q."
2. Discussion ensues (off-chain on forums to refine the idea).
3. Voting: Each token often equals one vote (though some DAOs use quadratic voting or other mechanisms to reduce whale influence). Voting might happen on-chain (if immediate execution is desired and to use tokens in smart contracts directly) or off-chain using signed messages (like Snapshot votes) for gas savings, where later a transaction can be executed if off-chain vote reached consensus.
4. Execution: If the vote passes, on-chain proposals can trigger their effects automatically. In other cases, a multi-sig of trusted members might execute the decision (some DAOs still rely on a multi-signature wallet for treasury, especially if they use off-chain voting).

Membership models: (Borrowing from the QuickNode guide) DAOs can be *token-based* or *share-based* quicknode.com.

- **Token-based membership:** Often permissionless – anyone who holds the governance token can participate. These DAOs are usually large and open (protocol DAOs, social DAOs). Tokens can be bought, earned, etc. This model can scale to thousands of members and works well for broad participation.

- **Share-based membership:** More permissioned – you gain membership by contributing work or tokens and receiving shares, or by being admitted. MolochDAO (a famous grants DAO) is an example: you join by putting some capital in, you get proportional shares, and you can exit at any time by "rage quitting" to withdraw your portion of assets. These DAOs are often used for investment clubs or where trust among members is a bit higher and they want to tightly control who's in the group (like a company's shareholders). Voting rights are based on shares and new members can be voted in.

These reflect different use cases: a globally open DeFi protocol vs a small club of investors.

Real-world governance vs DAO governance: For a beginner, it's useful to compare to something like a cooperative or condo association – those have members and votes on budgets, but often there's an elected board etc. DAOs try to eliminate unnecessary hierarchy by letting token holders directly vote on proposals. Some still form working groups or committees, but those can be accountable to on-chain votes (for example, a multisig that manages day-to-day funds might need periodic authorization via DAO vote).

DAO Governance Frameworks and Tools (Intermediate)

Launching a DAO is easier now thanks to established frameworks and tools:

- **Smart Contract Frameworks:** Aragon, DAOstack (Alchemy), and Moloch (and its many forks like DAOhaus) provide pre-built DAO contracts. For instance, **Aragon** offers modules for token voting, finance (treasury), and even a court for dispute resolution. A new Aragon DAO can be created with a few clicks: choose network, give it a name, set up your token or select a membership type, configure voting parameters (like voting duration, quorum, supermajority %, etc.), and deploy aragon.org. It's possible to spin up a DAO on testnets or sidechains very cheaply for experimentation.

- **Voting Systems:** The simplest is 1 token = 1 vote, majority wins. However, governance designers pay attention to:
  - **Quorum:** minimum % of total tokens that must participate for a vote to be valid, to prevent governance attacks by a small turnout.
  - **Thresholds:** e.g., a simple majority (>50%) or supermajority (>66%) depending on the decision type.
  - **Voting length:** proposals might be open for a few days to a week typically on-chain; off-chain Snapshot votes can be shorter since they don't cost gas for voters.
  - **Delegation:** Many DAOs encourage token holders to delegate their votes to more active participants (like how Compound and Uniswap have delegate systems). This creates a representative-like system to handle voter apathy.
  - **Quadratic Voting:** In some cases, to prevent whales from having outsized influence, quadratic voting can be used. It means the voting power is the square root of the tokens you hold (so to get twice the voting power, you need four times the tokens). This promotes wider voter distribution, but pure on-chain quadratic voting is vulnerable to Sybil (fake identity) attacks unless identity or one-person-one-vote is somehow enforced.
  - **Ranked choice or conviction voting:** There are experiments with more nuanced voting (ranking options, or conviction voting where continuous voting weight accumulates on options you support over time until you withdraw it).

- **Off-chain voting & on-chain execution:** A popular pattern: use **Snapshot** (off-chain, gasless voting platform) for polling token holders, then if it passes, a few multisig signers or a "DAO agent" contract executes the result on-chain. More advanced: **Compound's Governor Bravo** contract allows fully on-chain proposals where any token holder with enough delegates can propose, and token voting happens on-chain, then the contract itself calls the designated functions if it passes. This is truly autonomous but costs gas for voters and proposers.
- **Treasury Management:** DAOs hold treasuries often in multi-signature wallets (like Gnosis Safe) governed by proposals. Increasingly, tooling exists to manage funds, stream payments (Sablier can stream salary to contributors), and perform accounting.
- **Coordination Tools:** Beyond the blockchain, DAOs rely on platforms: forums (Discourse), chat (Discord/Telegram), project management (notion, etc.), and **Coordinape** (a tool where DAO members allocate "praise" or points to each other to decide reward splits for contributions). While not on-chain, these tools are vital to make decentralized coordination feasible.

Legal considerations: A very practical aspect – can a DAO sign a legal contract or hire employees in a legal sense? Right now, purely on-chain, a DAO is just an address. Some DAOs have formed legal wrappers (LLCs, cooperatives, etc.) to interface with the real world. For example, **The LAO** (a play on "The DAO") is a Delaware LLC that functions like a venture DAO but legally compliant. Wyoming created a law recognizing DAOs as a type of LLC. At the intermediate level, be aware that large DAOs often have a foundation or legal entity behind certain operations (for instance, to pay taxes or run a web domain), though the goal is to maximize what can be done trustlessly on-chain.

Challenges in DAO governance:

- **Voter Apathy:** Many governance tokens end up with low turnout. This can lead to governance attacks (someone accumulating tokens cheaply to force a vote through if quorum is low) or just ineffective governance. Delegation and incentives (like paying voters or requiring participation) are ways to combat this.
- **Whale Control:** If a few entities hold large percentages, the DAO could be decentralized in name but not in practice. Some DAOs have tried weighted systems or caps, but generally token distribution is crucial. Over time, projects try to decentralize further (e.g., early on founders/VCs hold a lot, but they might reduce influence as community grows).
- **Off-chain influence:** Not everything can be coded. DAOs sometimes face social issues: conflicts between factions, coordination failures, or even attacks like a 51% attack but for governance (someone buys majority of tokens just to misuse treasury – theoretically possible).
- **Security of Governance:** If a malicious proposal can pass (or if an attacker gets hold of private keys of delegates in a small DAO), they might drain funds. Some DAOs have built-in delay periods or escape hatches; for example, Compound has a time-lock on execution – after a proposal passes, there's a 2-day delay in which, if it was malicious, hopefully community notices and can react (maybe by social coordination to fork or something). Similarly, some DAOs limit what can be done without multiple steps of confirmation.

From a systems thinking perspective (linking to Dr. Goldston's interdisciplinary approach): DAO governance involves technology (smart contracts, tokens), economics (incentivizing participation, preventing plutocracy), law (legal status of a DAO), sociology (the community culture and trust), and even AI (some have mused about AI agents participating in DAO governance on behalf of humans or moderating discussions). It's a rich field of study and experimentation.

Legal and Game-Theoretic Considerations *(Advanced)*

At an advanced level, one examines DAOs as new kinds of organizations and their implications:

- **Jurisdiction and Regulation:** As mentioned, places like Wyoming treat DAOs as LLCs if registered. There's ongoing debate on how securities law applies to governance tokens (are they investment contracts? Many governance tokens also have expectations of profit or at least control over funds, which can raise regulatory eyebrows). Advanced readers would track evolving legal frameworks or case law. A notable case: the U.S. CFTC took enforcement action against the Ooki DAO (successor to bZx, a DeFi protocol that had an incident) by serving governance token holders through an online posting – raising question of DAO member liability.
- **Governance Attacks:** A theoretical attack: **51% governance attack** – if someone buys majority of tokens (perhaps gradually, if token price is low or liquidity is thin), they could pass proposals to drain treasury or maliciously change the protocol. Unlike 51% mining attacks (which are temporary unless you maintain hashing power), buying governance tokens gives persistent control until sold. The game theory is if a treasury has assets far exceeding the market cap of the governance token, it's potentially profitable to borrow money, buy tokens, loot treasury, etc. Some protocols put safeguards like requiring multiple voting rounds or hard-coding certain treasury operations to be restricted. This is a classic *economic security* issue.
- **Sybil resistance in DAOs:** Quadratic voting and other democratic ideals run up against the Sybil problem (one person creating many addresses to pretend to be many people). In token-based systems, capital is the barrier (which is Sybil-resistant to some degree, since making many accounts doesn't help if you don't have more tokens). There are projects like BrightID or Proof of Humanity trying to give

"one human, one identity" verification that could one day allow more human-centric voting rather than token-centric.
- **Game Theory of Voting:** Concepts like **voter turnout paradox**, **rational apathy** (if your vote is unlikely to swing an outcome and it costs effort, rationally you may not vote – common in large DAOs). Solutions could include quadratic funding of public goods to align incentives or paying voters (but that could cause bribery issues). Some have discussed mechanism like **commit-reveal voting** (to prevent voters just copying large token holders last minute) and **vote buying** markets (which can be negative, but others argue could be formalized).
- **Hierarchical DAOs and SubDAOs:** Large DAOs sometimes form sub-committees or sub-DAOs for specific tasks (for scalability of decision-making). For example, a main DAO might approve a yearly budget and high-level goals, then empower a sub-DAO or team to execute day-to-day. This mirrors corporate structure but ideally with more transparency and bottom-up control. Managing these relationships and ensuring sub-DAOs remain accountable is an advanced governance problem.
- **AI in Governance:** There's experimental thoughts on using AI to assist DAO governance, such as analyzing sentiment of proposals, automating some decisions, or even AI agents as members. One could imagine an AI that monitors the blockchain and automatically proposes optimizations (like adjusting fees) based on data, which token holders then vote on. This bleeds into our later AI integration discussion.

Case Study: Gemach DAO's Governance (tie-in): Earlier we looked at Gemach DAO as a DeFi project with AI agents. It's also a DAO. Suppose we consider how Gemach might govern its AI agent parameters or treasury. They might use a token (GMAC perhaps) and votes to decide adding a new feature to their GBot or adjusting loan parameters in GLend. Their challenge is interdisciplinary: they might need economic input (is this parameter sustainable), technical input (can our AI handle that), and community input (do users want it). This exemplifies why Dr. Goldston's systems thinking is key – governance decisions in Web3 often touch code, economics, and human factors simultaneously.

The Future of Governance: Advanced discussions often query if on-chain governance is truly effective or if we'll see more **algorithmic governance** (like more parts of the system that adjust automatically by formula rather than requiring votes) to reduce human error. For example, some DeFi protocols minimize governance, fearing it as a centralization vector (if governance can change everything, then controlling governance is akin to controlling the system). They prefer immutable or algorithm-driven parameters when possible.

Another view is **governance minimization** akin to *trust minimization* – keep critical functions automatic and only use governance for things that humans are uniquely needed for (like allocating funds to new projects where creativity is needed).

(Exercises – DAOs & Governance): 1. **Start a DAO (experiment):** Using a platform like Aragon or DAOhaus (if possible on a testnet), outline the steps to create a simple DAO for a club. What parameters would you set for voting period, quorum, etc., and why? 2. **Governance Attack Scenario:** Imagine a DAO that manages a treasury worth $1 million, and its governance token has a market cap of only $200k (perhaps because most tokens were airdropped and many haven't valued it much). Explain why this is dangerous. How could an attacker exploit this, and what could the DAO do to mitigate it (short of increasing token value)? 3. **Delegation Assignment:** In a large DAO, participation is low. Propose a delegation system: how would you encourage token holders to delegate? What qualities would you look for in a delegate (e.g., expertise, track record)? How might you prevent a scenario where all tokens delegate to one "super delegate," centralizing power again? 4. **Compare to Traditional Orgs:** List three differences between DAO governance and a traditional corporation's governance (shareholders, board of directors, executives). For each

difference, state one advantage and one disadvantage of the DAO approach. 5. **Philosophical Question:** Can code-based governance truly capture concepts of justice or equity? For example, if a certain minority group in a community holds very few tokens, their voice is small in a token-vote DAO. Is this an issue to be solved (perhaps via non-token mechanisms or weighted voting), or is it an acceptable trade-off since they had equal opportunity to acquire tokens? Discuss with respect to the idea "governance token = skin in the game," highlighting any alternative models you know (like one-person-one-vote DAOs or reputation systems).

Web3 Systems Thinking: An Interdisciplinary View (Advanced/Researcher)

We've covered the pillars of Web3 – blockchain tech, smart contracts, DeFi, DAOs – mostly from technical and economic angles. But Web3 is a **system** that spans multiple domains. This section adopts *Web3 Systems Thinking Theory* as developed by Dr. Justin Goldston, which encourages looking at Web3 through **interdisciplinary lenses**: economics, law, ethics, AI, governance, and even futurism (quantum computing, etc.). By analyzing Web3 as an interconnected whole, we can better design solutions that are sustainable and inclusive.

Economic and Incentive Systems

Token Economics (Tokenomics): Every Web3 project involves designing incentives via tokens. Economics comes into play to answer:

- How to distribute tokens fairly (initial airdrops vs. sales vs. mining)?

- What is the token's utility (governance, fee discounts, staking for security)? A token should ideally have a purpose that drives demand beyond speculation.
- Inflation vs. deflation: Some networks inflate supply to reward participants (like Ethereum had mining rewards, and now small staking rewards, plus fees partly burned making it deflationary at times). The design can mimic economic policy – e.g., Bitcoin's fixed cap of 21 million is deflationary long-term, which some liken to a digital gold standard.
- **Game theory** in incentives: Mechanism design is the field of creating rules for games (systems) that lead rational participants to a desired outcome. For example, in a liquidity pool, the fee rewards are mechanism design to attract liquidity providers; in governance, requiring tokens to vote is mechanism design to ensure voters have something at stake (so hopefully vote responsibly).
- **Market Dynamics:** Web3 often creates new markets (like prediction markets, or markets for computing power, etc.). Understanding supply and demand, market equilibrium, and economic externalities is crucial. For instance, if a network's token price crashes, will its security (for PoS) or usage be affected? Economics ties directly to technical security in PoS systems: if the token value is low, it's cheaper to buy 2/3 and attack.
- **Hybrid finance (HyFi) integration:** We mentioned how Current integrated with Acala current.com. From an economics perspective, HyFi aims to bring more capital efficiency – instead of banks giving 0.1% savings interest while DeFi could give 5%, HyFi might bridge that gap, potentially leading to a more efficient global allocation of capital (but also linking crypto volatility with traditional markets, which has systemic risk considerations).

Legal and Regulatory Perspectives

Web3 doesn't exist in a vacuum; laws and regulations worldwide are trying to catch up. Applying a legal lens:

- **Jurisdictional Arbitrage:** Some crypto projects move to crypto-friendly jurisdictions (like certain islands or Switzerland) to benefit from clearer or lenient laws. This mirrors how traditional companies incorporate in Delaware or offshore. But because blockchains are global, a DAO could have members everywhere, raising conflict of law issues (which country's regulations apply if something goes wrong?).
- **Compliance vs. Decentralization:** A fully decentralized protocol might be hard to regulate (there's no company to sue, no CEO to jail). But many Web3 projects start semi-centralized. We see a spectrum: on one end, Bitcoin – no central authority, likely unstoppable; on the other, a fintech app – completely in the scope of regulation. Many DeFI/DAO projects lie in between. Governments might hold core developers or big token holders accountable (as possibly indicated by the CFTC's approach to Ooki DAO).
- **Smart contracts and law:** If a contract is self-executing, is it a legal contract? Some jurisdictions are updating laws to recognize that *yes, code can represent an enforceable agreement* (with some caveats). Also, disputes: if a bug causes loss, legally who is responsible? There is an idea in crypto that *"code is law"* ted.com – meaning whatever the code does is the outcome, regardless of intent. But legal systems might not see it that way if human agreements or consumer protections are involved.
- **Intellectual Property:** Many Web3 projects are open source. But NFTs, for example, raise IP questions (buying an NFT might not confer copyright to the art, unless stated). Metaverse assets might need new IP frameworks.
- **Governance tokens as securities:** A big debate: if a token is used for governance and possibly profit (like a share), is it effectively a security (stock)? If yes, it should be registered and regulated. Projects like Uniswap chose to airdrop widely to avoid looking like a token sale, but the legal clarity is not fully there. The U.S. SEC has hinted many tokens are

securities, except maybe Bitcoin and some truly decentralized ones.
- **Privacy and KYC:** Decentralization often means pseudonymity. But regulations (AML, KYC) require identifying users in financial transactions to prevent crime. How to reconcile? Some think *zero-knowledge proofs* could allow compliance checks without revealing full identity (e.g., prove you're not on a sanctions list without revealing who you are). This is an active research and development area bridging law and cryptography.

Ethical and Social Considerations

Web3 proponents often speak of liberty, inclusion, and empowerment, but there are ethical questions:

- **Financial Inclusion vs. Risks:** Cryptocurrency can bank the unbanked (anyone with internet can hold Bitcoin), which is a positive. But it can also expose unsophisticated users to big risks (scams, volatility). What is the ethical duty of developers and community? Should there be safeguards or is caveat emptor (user responsibility) enough?
- **Environmental Impact:** Proof-of-Work was heavily criticized for energy usage. Ethereum's move to Proof-of-Stake cut energy by >99.9%. Many other blockchains use PoS or other low-energy methods. But Bitcoin still uses as much energy as some small countries ted.com for mining. Ethically, is it justifiable? Some argue yes (for strong security and as a driver of renewable energy development), others no (wasteful). This touches on sustainability, a key aspect of systems thinking (ensuring the system doesn't harm the environment or can sustain in the long run).
- **Decentralization and Personal Sovereignty:** Ethically, giving people control of their data and assets is empowering. But it also means if they lose their private key, they lose everything with no recourse. That's a usability and moral issue. Solutions like social recovery (designating friends to

help recover keys, as in Goldston's digital inheritance work arxiv.org) or multi-sig wallets help balance personal responsibility with safety nets.
- **Governance Equity:** As discussed, one-token-one-vote can concentrate power. Is there an ethical obligation to ensure more equitable governance (for example, giving users who contribute but aren't wealthy a voice)? Some DAOs experiment with **soulbound reputation tokens** – non-transferable tokens earned through contributions, used for voting to complement capital-based voting articlegateway.com. This could be more meritocratic.
- **Global inequality:** Will Web3 concentrate wealth or distribute it? Early adopters sometimes get disproportionately rich (e.g., early Bitcoin miners or Ethereum ICO participants). Web3 systems thinking would consider policies (like universal basic income tokens or community airdrops) to spread wealth creation. Projects like Gitcoin and retroactive public goods funding aim to use crypto wealth to fund open source and community goods, which is an ethical push within the space.

AI and Emerging Technology Perspectives

Web3 is now intersecting with other emerging tech:

- **Artificial Intelligence:** We'll cover AI integration in depth in the next chapter, but from a systems view: AI agents could participate in Web3 economies (trading, providing services) autonomously. Web3 can also provide data integrity and provenance for AI (like verifying data used to train AI). A fascinating concept is *Incentivized Symbiosis* arxiv.org – a term suggesting a social contract between humans and AI, encoded in Web3, where AI helps humans and gets rewarded in tokens, co-evolving together. This was explored by researchers inspired by Web3 principles arxiv.org.

- **Internet of Things (IoT):** Another integration – IoT devices using blockchains for coordination and security (e.g., a smart car paying automatically for charging or tolls with crypto; or devices forming mesh networks and being paid in tokens for providing connectivity).
- **Quantum Computing:** We'll discuss quantum in its own section later. Systems thinking must include planning for quantum-safe cryptography arxiv.org, as one part of the environment (technology capabilities) is changing. Also, quantum computing could eventually be used to run secure multiparty computations or accelerate certain blockchain operations (or break them if not prepared). Goldston's research foresaw the need to consider quantum impacts arxiv.org.
- **Education and Behavior:** Interdisciplinary view also means understanding how people learn about and use Web3. Psychology: what motivates users to trust a DAO over a company? How to design interfaces that encourage responsible behavior (like not falling for phishing)? Education is key – for Web3 to reach its potential, users need to grasp new concepts (seed phrases, etc.). So, systems thinking includes social science: user experience research, education programs (even blockchain in school curricula eventually).

Dr. Justin Goldston, being a professor and researcher, often emphasizes bringing these strands together:

- In his TEDx talks in 2019, he discussed blockchain's potential in various sectors from supply chain to daily life ted.com, essentially predicting that blockchain would not stay in the silo of finance, but permeate industries and improve them.
- He also likely highlighted *quantum computing* and *AI* as future factors in those talks thinkers360.com, demonstrating an early holistic view (blockchain doesn't exist alone, it will converge with AI and

IoT in the 4th Industrial Revolution, and we must be ready for quantum computers possibly challenging cryptography).
- In research, Goldston and collaborators applied frameworks like **Terror Management Theory** and **Logotherapy** to blockchain identity articlegateway.com, which is a perfect example of interdisciplinary thinking: using psychology and philosophy to interpret why people behave in Web3 (e.g., collecting NFTs to create meaning or legacy).

Summing up, a *systems thinking* approach to Web3 means:

- Recognizing the *interdependencies*: a change in protocol economics could affect user behavior and legal status; a regulatory change could drive innovation to more decentralization in tech, etc.
- Striving for holistic solutions: e.g., designing a DAO not just for efficient decision-making (tech view) or just for profit (economic view), but for long-term community health, compliance with necessary laws, fairness, etc.
- Continuous learning and adaptation: Web3 is experimental. Systems thinkers will monitor feedback (e.g., did a particular governance model lead to voter apathy? Did a token distribution create unintended speculation?). Then adjust the design.

(Exercises – Systems Thinking): 1. **Identify Interdependencies:** Pick a recent event or change in a Web3 project (for example, Ethereum adopting Proof-of-Stake, or a country adopting a crypto regulation). List the domains involved (tech, econ, legal, social) and describe at least one effect in each domain. How did they influence each other? 2. **Design Challenge:** Imagine you are creating a new Web3 platform for healthcare data (patients control their records via blockchain). Outline how you would approach this with systems thinking: consider technical requirements (security, privacy), legal (HIPAA compliance or equivalent), economic (who pays for the service, maybe token incentives for sharing anonymous data for research), ethical (consent management, preventing misuse), and social (getting hospitals and patients to actually use it). 3. **Web3 & AI Synergy:** Describe a scenario in 5 years where AI and Web3 might heavily interact in everyday life (e.g., an AI personal assistant that uses DAOs to hire services for you, or AI-created art being sold as NFTs and managed by a smart contract that pays the AI). What new questions does this raise? (Think legal – can AI own assets?; think economic – does AI undercut human jobs?; etc.) 4. **Quantum Threat Response:** Assume it's 2030 and a quantum computer is built that can break current cryptography. How might the Web3 community respond as a system? Consider the roles of researchers (to deploy post-quantum algorithms), governments (possibly intervening or funding defenses), blockchain networks (forking/upgrading), and end-users (might panic or need to migrate wallets). What does this scenario teach about resilience in system design? 5. **Bridging the Gap:** Choose one aspect where Web3 ideals clash with current reality (for example, privacy vs regulation, or decentralization vs user convenience). Propose a balanced approach that takes into account technical possibilities and policy considerations. For instance, can we create a DeFi identity solution that satisfies regulators (prove identity or reputation) *and* preserves user privacy using zero-knowledge proofs? Outline how that might work at a high level, showing understanding of both sides.

Case Studies in Web3: Innovation and Challenges in Action

To ground the concepts covered, this chapter dives into detailed case studies of Web3 projects and scenarios. We will examine **Gemach DAO**, **World Liberty Financial (WLF)**, and the involvement of political figures and memecoins in the crypto space. Through these case studies, we'll highlight successes, pitfalls, and quantitative insights where possible. Each case reflects a unique facet of Web3 – from technological innovation to social and political interplay.

Case Study 1: Gemach DAO – AI-Driven DeFi and Intelligent Agents

Overview: Gemach DAO is a community-driven DeFi project that stands out for integrating AI "Intelligent Agents" into its ecosystem. Gemach's mission is to *educate and empower people in decentralized finance through community-driven initiatives, tools, and open ecosystems* mirror.xyz. It operates as a DAO, meaning Gemach token holders can participate in governance and share in the platform's growth.

Products and Features: Gemach has developed a suite of DeFi tools:

- **GBot:** A powerful trading bot that works on multiple chains (EVM-based and Solana) gemach.io. It allows users to automate trading strategies, such as sniping newly launched tokens and avoiding sandwich attacks (a type of frontrunning).
- **Alpha Intelligence (AI) Platform:** This is Gemach's flagship AI integration. It lets users create, deploy, and manage **intelligent agents** in a decentralized environment docs.gemach.io. These agents can perform tasks like monitoring market trends, executing trades, and managing portfolios on behalf of users, according to predefined strategies. In the platform's **Build section**, users define agent properties and "skills" (which are like functions such as `get_trending_tokens`) by providing Python code or logic docs.gemach.io. Agents can even work in workflows of multiple agents communicating to accomplish complex tasks docs.gemach.io.
- **GLend and GLoans:** DeFi lending products (possibly akin to platforms like Liquity, given the reference to LUSD in resources gemach.io). There's mention of interest-free loans which suggests it may integrate with protocols like Liquity (where loans are interest-free but require collateral and a one-time fee).

- **GVault, GFund:** Likely treasury or fund management tools within the ecosystem.
- **Token Scanner (GScanner):** Tool to find latest token deployments – helpful for discovering new opportunities, which ties into their trading bot's purpose of quickly acting on new tokens.
- **Governance via Snapshot:** Gemach has a Snapshot for voting gemach.io, indicating they decentralize decisions to token holders.

Innovations – AI Agents in Web3: Gemach's claim to fame is pioneering the use of AI agents in DeFi:

- It arguably provides one of the first accessible interfaces for non-programmers to deploy AI bots on-chain. Users can define strategies in plain language or code, and the system handles the rest.
- These agents operate continuously ("available 24/7" as they tout) and can give users an edge by reacting to market conditions faster or more systematically than a human might.
- For example, an agent might be set to monitor decentralized exchange prices and automatically execute arbitrage when a price difference is detected. Or an agent might manage a user's liquidity provision, pulling funds out if impermanent loss risk becomes too high.
- Gemach's approach essentially brings *automation and personalization* to DeFi investing. Instead of just manually using DeFi platforms, a user can deploy their personal AI trader or risk manager.

Community and Education: True to their mission, Gemach emphasizes educating newcomers:

- They provide guides (e.g., a Beginner's Guide to Arbitrum gemach.io and security notes). They have active community channels (Twitter, Telegram, Discord).

- By lowering the technical barrier (via AI tools and user-friendly bots), they attract those who might not code but want to benefit from advanced strategies.

Tokenomics and DAO:

- Gemach likely has a token (GMAC perhaps, given a "Get Gemach Token" Uniswap link gemach.io). The token presumably is used for governance and possibly as an access or fee mechanism for their tools.
- As a DAO, proposals could include things like adjusting fee structures, choosing new features to develop, partnerships, or spending the treasury on marketing or audits.
- The intelligent agents themselves could be subject to governance: perhaps the community can vote to share particularly successful agent templates, or on limits if an agent could potentially cause systemic risk (for example, if many users run the same agent and it malfunctions, how to mitigate? The DAO might have a role in curating agents).

Numerical Analysis: While specific numbers for Gemach's usage aren't provided in the text we have, some possible metrics to consider:

- **User Base & Adoption:** We might look at how many agents have been created or how many active users in their platform. (Hypothetical example: Gemach might report "500 agents deployed with combined $X under management.")
- **Performance of Agents:** Are AI agents outperforming manual strategies? Perhaps Gemach publishes that an average agent yields Y% monthly returns in volatile markets – this could be an attractive stat (though would require careful analysis to avoid survivorship bias).
- **Treasury:** If Gemach did a token launch, how much did they raise, and how are they allocating it (e.g., 30% to development, etc.)?

- Without concrete data in the snippet, one can say Gemach's approach attracted enough attention that it co-authored academic work (we saw in search a mention of "Gemach D.A.T.A. I. Cooperation" in a research context researchgate.net, suggesting Gemach's concept of AI cooperation in DeFi was significant enough to be studied or presented academically).

Challenges: As a pioneering project, Gemach likely faces:

- **Technical Risk:** AI agents operating with real funds need to be robust. A bug in an agent's logic could cause losses. Gemach probably sandboxes agent code and has safety checks.
- **Market Risk:** Agents executing strategies don't guarantee profit; if markets move against the strategy (or many bots do the same thing causing crowding), users could lose money. Educating users on risk is important.
- **Adoption Hurdle:** Traditional DeFi users might be slow to trust AI with funds. Conversely, newcomers might trust too much. Striking the right balance in messaging and user control is delicate.
- **Competition:** As AI in trading is common in traditional finance (quant funds, etc.), similar ideas may spring up in Web3. But Gemach's early mover advantage and community focus help.

Significance: Gemach DAO illustrates Web3's composability: It combined **DeFi** (trading, lending) with **AI** (intelligent agents) under a **DAO governance** structure. This is a living example of interdisciplinary Web3 in action:

- Economics: Designing token incentives for people to share successful strategies maybe, or to provide liquidity so agents have funds to use.
- AI/Tech: Implementing a user-friendly AI on blockchain which involves computer science challenges.

- Governance: Letting a community decide on platform direction.
- Ethics: Ensuring AI decisions align with user's best interest (maybe implementing constraints to prevent an agent from taking ultra-high risks without user approval).

In essence, Gemach DAO shows how a Web3 project can push boundaries by merging technologies and empowering its community to drive innovation.

Case Study 2: World Liberty Financial (WLF) – When Politics Meets DeFi

Overview: World Liberty Financial (WLF) is a DeFi protocol founded in 2024 with a very high-profile affiliation – it's backed by members of the Trump family and associates. It brands itself as a platform for earning and borrowing crypto, but what sets it apart is the political dimension. Former U.S. President Donald Trump is involved, taking on the title of **"chief crypto advocate"**, his son **Barron Trump is dubbed the "DeFi visionary"**, and **Eric Trump and Donald Trump Jr. are "Web3 ambassadors"** of the project en.wikipedia.org. Such titles are unusual in the crypto industry and signal a marketing strategy leveraging political persona.

What WLF Does:

- It's described as a **decentralized finance protocol**, essentially a crypto exchange and lending platform where traders can invest and use crypto assets for borrowing and lending.
- It likely has its own token, presumably **$WLFI**, which might be used for governance or profit-sharing on the platform. (Indeed, Coingecko snippet refers to "World Liberty Financial is the DeFi project backed by ... and its token WLFI" coingecko.com).
- WLF introduced a concept of a **"strategic token reserve"** to stabilize crypto markets

blockhead.co. They announced creating a Macro Strategy reserve to *"bolster leading projects like..."* (the quote cuts, but presumably like Bitcoin, etc.) and reduce volatility blockhead.co. This sounds like WLF aspires to act like a crypto central bank or sovereign wealth fund, accumulating major crypto (BTC, ETH, etc.) to support the market.

Political Involvement and Impact:

- Donald Trump's involvement is unprecedented — a former (and possibly future) President officially leading a crypto venture. This has drawn massive attention and also skepticism. It blurs lines between politics and crypto finance.
- Trump's social media (Truth Social) and rallies have given crypto shoutouts; for instance, he changed stance from critical to supportive recently blockworks.co. WLF could be partly an outcome of that shift, aligning with a political narrative of embracing crypto innovation (and perhaps fundraising through it).
- The **Trump brand** likely attracted many supporters to buy the token or join the platform, not purely on technical merit but loyalty or speculation on the Trump effect.

Numerical Highlights:

- **Holdings:** As per Reuters and Blockhead sources, WLF had significant holdings of other cryptos:
    - It *"possesses 30 million TRX, valued at $7.43 million"* blockhead.co. TRX is Tron's token; this hints at an alliance with Justin Sun (Tron founder). Indeed, Justin Sun invested heavily in WLF.
    - WLF also apparently bought large amounts of ETH, LINK, AAVE with USDC, causing price surges in those assets. Specifically: *"acquired 2,631 ETH, 41,335 LINK, and 3,357 AAVE"* according to one report.

- **Justin Sun's Investment:** Justin Sun spent at least $75 million on WLF's token, becoming the largest outside investor. He also joined WLF as an advisor after this investment. This injection was huge relative to many DeFi projects and gave WLF a hefty war chest.
- **Market Reaction:** Tron's price climbed ~29% (to $0.25) after Sun's involvement and WLF's Tron purchases. This shows how WLF's activities impacted crypto markets. It also raises concerns: a politically-connected entity coordinating with a crypto mogul to possibly prop up certain assets — this could be seen as savvy market making or as manipulation, depending on perspective.
- **Ethics and Conflict Concerns:** Sun's $75M into a Trump-affiliated project was noted to raise conflict of interest questions. If Trump has political power again, an advisor like Sun might benefit from favorable policies. WLF being led by a President also begs: if regulatory or economic policy could be influenced in ways that benefit WLF or its holdings, that's an ethics issue. Critics have called it *"a self-serving obsession"*, though supporters see it as positive for mainstream crypto adoption.

WLF Token ($WLFI):

- Launch and Price: It's implied people purchased WLFI, perhaps expecting it to moon thanks to the Trump name. Indeed, Mike Dudas (a known crypto figure) bought over 140,000 WLFI tokens before Trump's inauguration (per Blockhead), indicating speculation by insiders.
- Governance: WLFI holders have a say in product and marketing decisions, a somewhat novel feature to advertise in a politically tied project. That suggests a DAO-like element: they try to frame it as a community-run thing rather than just Trump-run. However, given the family's titles and presumably large token holdings, how decentralized is it in practice is unclear.

- Performance: If one source (reddit or such) indicated numbers: possibly WLFI saw a pump and volatility. For instance, if Justin Sun bought in, maybe the price spiked, then with scrutiny or market sentiment it might have fluctuated heavily. (We saw references to memecoins named after figures—perhaps WLFI trades like a memecoin partly, driven by hype more than fundamentals).

Regulatory and Governance Challenges:

- As of late 2024, Trump's platform also shifting focus to crypto services was noted. There's mention of Trump Media & Technology Group (the social media company) planning crypto financial services. This convergence means regulators (SEC, etc.) will be watching closely. Any misstep could invite enforcement (especially since Trump's enterprises are often under legal microscope).
- WLF trying to form alliances with financial institutions to add tokenized assets to the reserve shows a strategy to intertwine with traditional finance. But banks partnering with a Trump crypto venture could face reputational risk or regulatory caution.

Memecoin and Political Hype:

- WLF could be considered a memecoin with utility – memecoin in that it's propelled by a celebrity personality. It parallels how **Elon Musk and Dogecoin** interact, but here it's a formal project with the personality at the helm.
- Political memecoins historically: There were coins like MAGAcoin, TrumpCoin, Let's Go Brandon (LGB) coin. LGBcoin especially had a saga: it sponsored a NASCAR, then got banned by NASCAR, and its value crashed 99% reddit.com marketwatch.com. This shows risk: hype can drive a token up, but lack of substance or external support can crash it. WLFI tries to position with substance (a

platform and reserves), but it's unclear if that will sustain usage or if interest is mostly because of Trump.
- JD Vance (an Ohio Senator allied with Trump) ironically had a memecoin named after him (VANCE token) trading at fractions of a cent coinmarketcap.com. That token is likely just a joke and not endorsed by him, but it reflects how any political figure's name becomes fodder for memecoins. These tokens often have near-zero real value but serve as commentary or speculation vehicles.

World Liberty Financial's Role:

- **Adoption:** On one hand, WLF has probably brought new people into crypto – Trump's base might have started looking at crypto because "Trump's crypto project" made headlines. If even a fraction of his supporters decided to learn to use a wallet to get WLFI, that is significant for adoption (although some might use a custodian or simplified app WLF provides).
- **Global Perspective:** The involvement of Justin Sun (a Chinese entrepreneur) and Tron (popular in Asia) with an American political project is a twist. It indicates Web3's global nature – alliances form across borders, perhaps circumventing traditional geopolitical boundaries in finance.
- **Governance in Practice:** If we treat WLF as a DAO-like entity because of token governance, it's an experiment of mixing political hierarchy with decentralized governance. In practice, likely the Trumps and close partners hold a majority of influence (so more like a corporation with shareholders where the Trumps are majority shareholders and executives). However, they might perform some votes to maintain a decentralized facade. It's unclear if, say, WLFI token holders could outvote Trump on a proposal – probably unlikely due to distribution and the fact that the brand is tied to him.

Controversies and Criticisms:

- Some have called the venture murky or raised scam alarms. Fast Company called out "scammers flooding Trump's new crypto exchange" early on en.wikipedia.org – perhaps fake tokens or imitation sites trying to capitalize on hype, which is a risk to consumers.
- Ethics: The New York Times and others likely scrutinized how Trump was launching this while planning a run for office en.wikipedia.org. Are donors being sold tokens? Does this circumvent campaign finance laws if supporters buy tokens thinking it helps Trump? They have to be careful to separate WLF from campaign fundraising explicitly.

Outcome (Speculative):

- If WLF succeeds, it could set a precedent for political figures launching tech ventures, which could either bring mainstream legitimacy to crypto or conversely bring more populist volatility.
- If it fails or has a major issue, it could become a high-profile cautionary tale, possibly invoking regulatory crackdowns ("if even a President's project had issues, we need to regulate!" some might say).

Case Study 3: Politics and Memecoins – Trump, JD Vance, and the Meme Economy

This case looks at how political figures and internet meme culture intersect with crypto tokens. We've touched on Trump via WLF, but also consider:

- **Trump's NFTs:** In late 2022, Donald Trump launched a series of NFT trading cards (digital collectibles of himself in various heroic poses) at $99 each. 45,000 NFTs sold out rapidly (~$4.45M raised) and became a media sensation. This was arguably the first major U.S. politician to directly monetize via crypto tokens (NFTs) ted.com. The floor prices on secondary markets jumped, proving both the draw of his

fan base and speculators. However, values later fluctuated; still, it introduced thousands to NFTs who might not have cared before.
- **JD Vance:** A U.S. Senator known to be crypto-friendly (pushed legislation to clarify SEC/CFTC roles blockworks.co). JD Vance hasn't launched a coin, but someone created a **JD Vance (VANCE) token** on Solana dexscreener.com. This token trades at an infinitesimal price ($0.000002, essentially zero market cap) binance.com. It's likely a joke – reflecting his name in the crypto realm with no official backing. Such memecoins exist for many public figures, often as commentary or to ride name recognition.
- **Let's Go Brandon (LGB) Coin:** This was created by supporters of the anti-Biden slogan "Let's Go Brandon". It briefly got mainstream attention when NASCAR driver Brandon Brown announced LGBcoin sponsorship for his car. NASCAR then rejected the sponsorship due to political concerns cbssports.com. LGBcoin soared to a market cap of around $6.5M but later crashed over 99% to virtually nothing reddit.com. Many holders lost money, illustrating how memecoins tied to fleeting political memes carry extreme risk. The project also faced a lawsuit (alleging misleading investors) marketwatch.com.
- **MAGA Coin / TrumpCoin:** There have been coins named after MAGA or Trump since 2016. None were official, and many ended up as pump-and-dump schemes or fizzled out.

Memecoin Characteristics:

- *No intrinsic value:* They usually have no utility beyond trading. Value is driven by community sentiment and publicity.
- *High volatility:* Spikes during media buzz, then deep crashes (as seen with LGBcoin).
- *Community & Narrative:* Memecoins often form communities (like r/WallStreetBets did around stocks, crypto has Telegram/Discord groups). The narrative (be it anti-

establishment, or in-joke) is a key driver. For example, Dogecoin thrived on fun and altruism (tipping, sponsoring a NASCAR ironically).
- *Celebrities Shilling:* Elon Musk's tweets famously send Doge prices swinging. Similarly, a tweet from a politician can pump related tokens even if they aren't endorsing them (people speculate anyway).

Political Impact on Crypto Adoption:

- Politicians embracing crypto (like Miami's Mayor Suarez launching MiamiCoin, or NY Mayor Adams taking paycheck in Bitcoin) signal to the public that crypto is legitimate. JD Vance being crypto-friendly suggests future laws that are accommodating, which can influence market confidence.
- On the other side, some political involvement is purely opportunistic or for fundraising. Observers worry some could use tokens as unregulated campaign contributions.
- Memecoins named after politicians can embarrass them if things go wrong (imagine a coin named after a candidate that rugs investors, opponents could use that in campaigns).

Milei and Memecoins (International example): As a footnote on politics and crypto: In Argentina, newly elected President Javier Milei is pro-crypto. A memecoin named LIBRA (unrelated to Facebook's Libra) gained hype as supposedly Milei-endorsed (though he denied it). On-chain data linked its deployer to another token named MELANIA (perhaps referencing Melania Trump) blockhead.co. When Milei distanced himself, LIBRA's price plummeted and it hurt some investors. This showcases that global political waves also create meme tokens; and misinformation or assumptions can drive a token's boom and bust.

Analysis:

- **Market Cap and Volume:** Memecoins often have low market caps but can have high % gains/losses. They're prone to pumps (sometimes orchestrated in chat groups)

and dumps. For example, a memecoin might go from $10,000 market cap to $1,000,000 (a 100x) in days with just a few tweets mention, then back down.
- **Number of Holders:** These tokens often have many holders who put in very small amounts (fun money). E.g., 10,000 holders each with $100 can drive a cap to $1M. If one whale holds a big portion, that's a danger sign – many memecoins see one or few wallets holding majority of supply (often the creators), who can dump.
- **Regulatory Reaction:** Generally, regulators haven't cracked down on pure memecoins unless fraud is involved. But if a politician was directly involved in a token that lost people money, there could be investigations.

Trump's Changing Crypto Stance:

- Historically Trump said he wasn't a fan of Bitcoin (2019). By 2023-24, he not only launched NFTs but also reportedly holds ETH (from NFT sales) and possibly BTC. Politically, the Republican platform in 2024 is turning pro-crypto, vowing to end the "un-American crypto crackdown" blockworks.co. This pivot likely influenced many followers to reconsider crypto. So, beyond memecoins, the political talk around crypto (positive or negative) can significantly shift public sentiment. For instance, *after Trump's NFT success*, other politicians might consider similar ventures, or at least acknowledge the voter segment that cares about crypto.

Memecoins as Cultural Barometer:

- The existence of memecoins for political memes shows how crypto markets react in *real-time to cultural moments*. It's both fascinating and dangerous – as it allows anyone to monetize a catchphrase with little oversight.
- They also reflect a sort of protest or enthusiasm: e.g., creation of "FJB" (F*** Joe Biden) coin or "PEPE" (based on a meme frog sometimes tied to political fringe) which soared

in 2023, show subcultures using tokens as an expression of identity or satire.

Conclusion on this Case:

- Political figures are increasingly part of the crypto narrative, whether through direct projects or community-driven tokens.
- This intersection can drive adoption and innovation (like MiamiCoin funding city projects) but also scams and speculation.
- It underscores the need for education: new entrants drawn by a famous name need to understand not all that glitters is gold in crypto. A token with a familiar name is not inherently safer.
- It also emphasizes that Web3 is not just technical – it's deeply social. Memes and personalities can create and destroy millions in value overnight, a reminder that psychological factors are as important as code in this space.

(Exercises – Case Studies): 1. **Gemach's AI Agents:** If 100 users each deploy an agent with a $1,000 portfolio, and on average the agents achieved a 5% monthly return through automated strategies, what is the collective profit after one month and what does this imply about Gemach's impact (quantitatively and qualitatively)? Also, list two potential risks these agents face that the users should be aware of. 2. **WLF Strategic Reserve:** WLF created a reserve with assets like BTC, ETH, TRX, etc. Explain how having such a reserve could *reduce* volatility (e.g., acting as a buyer of last resort in market crashes) and how it could potentially *increase* volatility or create market distortions (e.g., if people speculate on which coins WLF will support). 3. **Token Governance in WLF:** If WLFI token holders vote on marketing decisions, formulate a hypothetical proposal and outcome: e.g., "Proposal: Spend 10% of reserve to list WLFI on a top exchange." What factors would holders consider (token value boost vs. reducing reserve) and what conflicts of interest might arise (insiders dumping after listing)? 4. **Memecoin Aftermath:** Using the LGBcoin example: it peaked at $6.5M and then went to ~$10k

(99.85% drop). If an average investor put $1,000 at peak, how much would they have after the crash? What lessons about market fundamentals vs hype does this illustrate? 5. **Political Crypto Strategy:** Suppose you are an advisor to a political figure who wants to engage with crypto to boost a campaign. Outline two approaches: one leveraging Web3 positively (like Miami's approach of creating a city token to fund public goods) and one that is more dubious (like launching a token mainly to raise money with vague promises). Evaluate the risks and rewards of each, and recommend the ethical path forward.

Blockchain Security, Cryptography, and Quantum Computing

Security is the bedrock of Web3. This chapter focuses on the cryptographic foundations that secure blockchains and smart contracts, examines how they withstand attacks, and looks ahead to the looming threat (and potential opportunity) of quantum computing in the Web3 context. We will also discuss how Web3 systems are evolving to maintain security against future challenges.

Cryptographic Foundations of Web3 *(Advanced)*

Web3 systems rely on several fundamental cryptographic primitives:

- **Hash Functions:** (e.g., SHA-256, Keccak-256) – Used in virtually every blockchain for linking blocks (Merkle trees and block hashes) and for addresses (Ethereum addresses are derived via Keccak). Hashes ensure data integrity: if any bit of a transaction or block changes, the hash changes unpredictably, alerting everyone that tampering occurred. Hash functions are designed to be one-way and collision-resistant (finding two different inputs that produce the same hash is astronomically unlikely). For example, Bitcoin's Proof-of-Work requires finding a hash with a certain number

of leading zeros; this property comes from the hash's pseudorandomness deloitte.com.
- **Digital Signatures:** (e.g., ECDSA for Bitcoin/Ethereum, Ed25519 for some newer networks) – They ensure **authenticity** and **non-repudiation** of transactions. When you sign a transaction with your private key, anyone can use your public key to verify the signature is valid and corresponds to your address, without knowing your private key. This means only the holder of the private key (the legitimate owner) could have initiated the transaction. Cryptography behind ECDSA involves elliptic curve math; the security assumption is that the **elliptic curve discrete logarithm problem** is hard (given P and aP on a curve, it's infeasible to find a).
- **Merkle Trees:** Used to organize transactions in a block. A Merkle tree takes all transaction hashes, pairs them and hashes them, repeating until a single root hash remains. This **Merkle root** is included in the block header. It allows efficient proofs of inclusion: a *Merkle proof* is a short sequence of hashes that any node can use to verify a particular transaction is in the block without downloading all transactions. This is critical for lightweight clients (SPV in Bitcoin).
- **Zero-Knowledge Proofs (ZKPs):** Although not in early blockchains, ZKPs are becoming important in Web3. Protocols like Zcash use zk-SNARKs to enable private transactions (proving that a transaction is valid without revealing the amounts or addresses involved). Ethereum layer-2 networks and privacy layers are adopting ZKPs for scalability and privacy, respectively. ZKPs are advanced cryptography where one can prove knowledge of a secret or correctness of an execution without revealing the secret or execution itself.
- **Secure Hashing of Public Keys:** Many chains hash public keys to form addresses (e.g., Bitcoin uses double SHA-256 and RIPEMD160). This adds an extra layer of security: even if one day a quantum computer could derive a private key

from a public key, if an address is only known via its hash (until it's used), the public key isn't revealed until the owner spends from that address. Bitcoin's UTXO best practice is *use new addresses each time* so that any one public key is exposed only when it's about to no longer hold funds (reducing window of vulnerability).

Consensus and Sybil Resistance: Cryptography also underpins consensus:

- Proof-of-Work's difficulty relies on hash preimage resistance (i.e., miners can't cheat the system without doing the work, because finding a valid hash is brute force).
- Proof-of-Stake uses cryptographic sortition (pseudo-randomly selecting validators weighted by stake using verifiable random functions or hash entropy from prior blocks) and BLS signatures in some protocols (like Ethereum 2 uses BLS aggregate signatures to have thousands of validators sign off on blocks efficiently).
- Sybil resistance means making it expensive to create identities. PoW makes identities (mining nodes) costly via computing power; PoS via requiring stake. Both use crypto (hash puzzles or staking transactions) to enforce that cost.

Attacks and Defenses:

- **51% Attack:** If an attacker gains >50% of mining power (PoW) or stake (PoS), they can create an alternate blockchain history (e.g., double spend transactions). Cryptography doesn't prevent this – it's an economic security model – but cryptography ensures honest parties can always detect a fork. The real defense is decentralization (make it infeasible to get that majority). In PoS, slashing provides some deterrent (an attacker would lose a lot of stake if caught trying equivocation).
- **Private Key Security:** The cryptography is strong (e.g., 256-bit keys have an astronomically large keyspace). The weak

link tends to be human: if you expose your seed phrase or use an insecure wallet, the crypto won't save you. That's why hardware wallets are recommended (they keep keys isolated) and why schemes like social recovery are being explored arxiv.org so losing a key isn't catastrophic.
- **Smart Contract Vulnerabilities vs. Crypto:** Most hacks in DeFi are due to code bugs or economic logic issues, not failures of cryptography. One exception: random number generation using block data was exploited (because it's not truly random). Now best practice is to use oracles or commit-reveal for randomness.
- **Double Spend and Finality:** In PoW, there's probabilistic finality – the chance of reorg drops as more blocks are mined on top. Cryptographically, each additional block confirms the previous by including its hash. In PoS BFT consensus, cryptography (signatures by 2/3 validators) can give immediate finality: if a supermajority signs a block at epoch checkpoint, that block is final and cannot be changed unless those validators collude and slash themselves.

Elliptic Curves and Addresses Example (Bitcoin):

- Bitcoin address creation:
    1. Generate a 256-bit private key.
    2. Compute the elliptic curve public key (a point on secp256k1 curve).
    3. Hash the public key (SHA-256 then RIPEMD160) to get a 160-bit key hash.
    4. Add version byte (0x00 for mainnet) and compute a checksum (first 4 bytes of double SHA256 of the data).
    5. Append checksum, then encode in Base58. That's your address (e.g., 1A1zP1...).
- The probability of someone randomly guessing your 256-bit private key is $1/2^{256}$ – essentially zero. For perspective, $2^{256} \approx 1.16 \times 10^{77}$, which is more than the number of atoms in the observable universe

by many orders of magnitude. This is why brute force is impossible.
- However, we did see some issues: e.g., a flaw in random number generation in early Bitcoin wallets led to some keys being guessable. If the RNG is bad (low entropy), that's a vulnerability. Cryptography assumes certain things like secure key generation.

Quantum Computing: Threats and Opportunities (Advanced/Researcher)

Quantum computers, if they reach sufficient size and stability, pose a significant threat to current cryptographic schemes:

- **Shor's Algorithm:** Invented by Peter Shor in 1994, this quantum algorithm can factor large integers and compute discrete logarithms in polynomial time. This directly breaks RSA and ECDSA (and ECDH) because their security is based on the difficulty of factoring or discrete logs. A sufficiently powerful quantum computer could derive a private key from a public key relatively quickly. For Bitcoin/Ethereum, that means any address where the public key is known (i.e., has made a transaction) could be compromised. Also, an attacker could forge digital signatures.
- **Grover's Algorithm:** A quantum search algorithm that gives a quadratic speed-up for brute force search. It could affect symmetric cryptography (like hash functions or AES) by effectively halving the security bit-length. SHA-256 (256-bit) might have its security reduced to ~128-bit, which is still quite secure. But weaker hashes or shorter keys might need upgrading. Grover's algorithm means we might eventually prefer using SHA-512 or doubling key lengths for symmetric encryption.
- **Timeline:** Experts estimate that a cryptographically relevant quantum computer (able to break 2048-bit RSA or 256-bit ECC) is still years if not a decade or more away

tandfonline.com utimaco.com. However, progress is unpredictable. The rule of thumb is: plan transitions now, because upgrading cryptography across decentralized networks takes time.

Blockchain Vulnerabilities to Quantum:

- Bitcoin: Addresses that haven't spent (public key not revealed, only hashed) are safe for now. But addresses that have spent once (public key revealed in the spending transaction) are vulnerable in the future. Satoshi's large stash, interestingly, might be safer because those coins never moved (public keys not known). But if someone re-uses an address or uses a vanity address (some early ones did weak stuff), they could be picked off. Also mining could be affected: if quantum computers can compute hashes faster (Grover gives sqrt speedup, but PoW is a parallelizable problem; still, quantum might not help much in hashing because of need for many parallel qubits).
- Ethereum: It uses Keccak-256 and ECDSA – same issues for account keys. Additionally, many smart contracts rely on crypto (e.g., certain DeFi protocols use elliptic curve pairings or other math) which could be at risk.
- If an attacker had a QC today, worst-case they could target high-value addresses (exchange cold wallets, DAO treasuries) and steal funds by deriving keys. Also, they could potentially fake blocks or messages if they can break signatures of validators or miners.

Post-Quantum Cryptography (PQC): These are crypto algorithms believed to be secure against quantum attacks, running on classical computers (no quantum tech needed to use them). NIST has been running a competition to standardize PQC; by 2022 they announced some winners (like CRYSTALS-Dilithium for signatures, CRYSTALS-Kyber for encryption). Blockchains can migrate to PQC gradually:

- New address types could use PQC-based public keys (like lattice-based signatures). For instance, there are proposals for Bitcoin to implement Lamport signatures or other PQC schemes for those who want quantum resistance at the cost of bigger signatures.
- One challenge: PQC keys and signatures are often larger. This could bloat blockchain data. But as tech improves and with careful choice (like using hash-based signatures XMSS or SPHINCS+ for one-time uses), it can be manageable.
- **QRL (Quantum Resistant Ledger):** An altcoin that already uses XMSS (hash-based sigs) to be quantum-safe from the ground up. It proves it's feasible, though not widely adopted.
- Ethereum research has considered how to introduce new signature schemes in future forks if needed.

Quantum as an Opportunity:

- **Quantum-secure blockchains:** Projects could differentiate by being quantum-safe, attracting e.g. governmental or long-term investors worried about quantum.
- **Quantum computing for good:** On the flip side, quantum tech could improve blockchains. For example, quantum random number generators could provide true randomness beacons for on-chain use. Quantum communication (QKD - Quantum Key Distribution) could secure validator communication beyond classical encryption.
- In a more futuristic sense, one might imagine a quantum blockchain (though the term is often misused in marketing). Possibly using quantum states to reach consensus or store information with quantum entanglement for instant sync (that's very speculative and far-off).

Transition Strategy:

- The Web3 community takes this seriously. Bitcoin developers have discussed a "quantum ready" upgrade in the coming decade (likely switching to a quantum-safe

signature scheme). The challenge: how to do that without stranding old coins whose owners are inactive or lost keys? One idea: after a certain year, transactions with old sigs might require an extra proof they weren't quantum hacked (maybe a kind of time-locked or multi-sig condition).
- Ethereum could allow smart contracts to verify PQC signatures (even now one could write a contract to require both an ECDSA sig and a Dilithium sig to move funds, providing forward security).
- As Goldston's work highlights, planning for AI and quantum is part of long-term strategy arxiv.org. Projects serious about long-term viability have R&D in these areas now.

Analogy: Think of current crypto as a castle protected by unimaginable mathematical moats. Quantum computing is like the advent of gunpowder in medieval times – it could suddenly make those high walls less effective. The castle has to evolve (maybe build bunkers, use new materials). PQC are those new defenses (like designing fortifications that can withstand cannon fire).

Current Actions:

- In 2022, the Bitcoin community saw academic papers about quantum attacks being slightly overblown unless certain scale reached. But also ideas like a "vault" contract where you have a pre-signed transaction to move funds to a safe address if someone tries a quantum spend.
- Governments are already migrating their own cryptography to PQC (the US NSA, etc.). Web3 will likely follow suit, probably starting with those who secure extremely valuable assets or nation-state-level interest.

(To illustrate, some numbers: If a QC with 4096 logical qubits running at a high clock could break secp256k1 in maybe hours, how many addresses could it target per day? Possibly not too many at first. Attackers would logically go for biggest bounties. It's expected *that well before that point, the network will have transitioned or users will have moved funds to new addresses.)*

In conclusion, cryptography is both the shield and the Achilles heel of Web3 – a strength as long as assumptions hold. The community must remain vigilant and proactive to upgrade that shield as technology advances.

(Exercises – Security & Quantum): 1. **Collision Resistance:** Explain why a collision in a hash function could be dangerous for a blockchain. For instance, if someone found two different transactions that hash to the same value, how could that undermine the integrity of Merkle trees or proof-of-work? (Hypothetical since SHA-256 collisions are not known, but assume.) 2. **ECDSA Break Scenario:** Imagine it's 2035 and a quantum computer can derive private keys from 256-bit public keys in a day. Alice has an old Ethereum account she hasn't used since 2020 with a big balance, public key is on-chain from when she last sent ether. Describe what an attacker could do and what Alice should do preemptively before 2035 to secure her funds. 3. **Design a PQC Transition:** Propose a backward-compatible upgrade for Bitcoin to introduce quantum-resistant addresses. How might you allow existing coin owners to move to new addresses? How do you deal with coins whose owners are inactive? (Consider maybe an alerting mechanism or an incentive to move.) 4. **Quantum vs. Mining:** If a quantum computer gives a miner effectively a quadratic speedup in hashing (Grover's algorithm), how would that impact the mining competition? If one miner had such a quantum advantage and others didn't, what fraction of blocks could they dominate theoretically? (Discuss in terms of hash rate advantage.) 5. **Sociology of Security:** Not strictly technical – why do you think many users still fall for phishing and give away their private keys, despite the unbreakable cryptography protecting them otherwise? What measures (technological or educational) could Web3 implement to reduce human-targeted security breaches (consider things like social recovery wallets, multi-factor auth with hardware wallets, user education gamification, etc.)?

Hands-On Web3: Building and Contributing (Practical Guides)

This chapter provides practical, step-by-step guidance on participating in and building Web3 applications. From creating a wallet to writing a simple smart contract and launching a DAO, these hands-on guides aim to empower you to apply the concepts learned. Even if you're not a developer, understanding the process will deepen your insight into how Web3 systems are implemented.

Getting Started: Wallet Setup and Basic Transactions (Beginner)

1. **Setting Up a Wallet:** To interact with Web3, you need a crypto wallet. Two user-friendly options:
    - **Mobile Wallet (Custodial):** E.g., Coinbase Wallet app or Blockchain.com app. These manage your keys for you (not your keys, not your coins – but easier for beginners). Simply install, follow sign-up, and you have an Ethereum/Bitcoin address to send/receive.
    - **Browser Extension Wallet (Self-custodial):** MetaMask is the popular choice for Ethereum and compatible networks. Install the MetaMask extension. It will prompt you to create a new wallet:
        - Set a strong password for the extension.
        - MetaMask will then give you a **12-word seed phrase**. **Write this down on paper** (don't save digitally) and keep it safe. This seed phrase can restore your wallet if your computer is lost. Losing it means losing access; someone else seeing it means they can steal your funds.
        - Confirm the seed by selecting the words in order to ensure you backed it up.

- Once done, MetaMask will show your account (address). By default, it's on Ethereum mainnet. You can switch to testnets or other networks (like Polygon, BSC) as needed by adding their RPC info.
2. **Obtaining Testnet Funds:** It's wise to practice on a testnet (like Ethereum's Goerli or Sepolia) so you don't risk real money.
    - Use a faucet service (a website that gives free testnet ETH). For Goerli, you might tweet your address and paste link to a faucet, or use community faucets. In MetaMask, switch network to Goerli, copy your address, and request faucet drip. Soon, you'll have some test-ETH in your wallet.
    - Confirm you see the balance (e.g., 0.2 Goerli ETH).
3. **Sending a Transaction:** Let's send some test ETH to another address:
    - In MetaMask, click "Send", enter the recipient address (could be your second account or a friend's).
    - Enter an amount (e.g., 0.1 test ETH).
    - Gas fee: MetaMask will suggest a gas fee. On testnets this is low, on mainnet it could be a few dollars in ETH. Click confirm.
    - You'll see the transaction pending. After a few seconds or minutes (depending on network speed and gas), it will complete. You can click the transaction in MetaMask to view it on a block explorer (like Etherscan).
    - On Etherscan (for testnet, goerli.etherscan.io), you'll see details: from, to, amount, gas used, etc. This transparency is what we discussed earlier – everything is public.
4. **Using a Web3 dApp:**
    - Let's try a simple one: a Uniswap trade on a testnet or a simple lending on a testnet platform.
    - For Uniswap on mainnet, you'd go to app.uniswap.org, connect MetaMask, then you can swap for tokens. On testnet, you could find a smaller

DEX or deploy your own (later in smart contract section).
- Alternatively, try a faucet dApp: There are faucet dApps where you click a button to get tokens (this initiates a contract call to mint you test tokens).
- When you connect MetaMask, a prompt appears "Allow this site to connect to your wallet?" – always verify you trust the site. Click connect.
- Now the dApp can read your address and balance (with your permission) and present options. If you click "Get tokens" or "Swap", MetaMask will pop up a transaction request describing what the contract call does (sometimes just technical method names). Confirm it if it looks right. Then wait for confirmation.
- Through this, you learn how signing works – the dApp can propose transactions but only you (with your private key via MetaMask) can authorize them.

5. **Safety Tips:**
   - Never share your private key or seed. No legit support will ask for it.
   - Double-check addresses you send to (one letter off and funds could go to someone else or be lost).
   - Be careful with phishing: only download MetaMask from official site, and only connect your wallet to reputable dApps. If a random site asks you to sign a weird message, think twice.
   - For developers: keep separate wallets for testing and small funds vs. holding large funds.

By now, you've effectively done basic Web3 interactions: manage keys, send a transaction, and interact with a smart contract via a dApp UI.

Writing and Deploying a Simple Smart Contract *(Intermediate)*

Let's create a simple Ethereum smart contract using Solidity and deploy it to a test network.

Contract Goal: A basic storage contract that allows anyone to set and get a number. (It's a common "Hello World" of Solidity.)

1. **Setup Development Environment:** Easiest is using Remix, an online IDE at `remix.ethereum.org`. It runs in the browser, no installation needed.
    - Open Remix. On the left, create a new file `SimpleStorage.sol`.
    - Ensure the environment is "Solidity" and compiler version is set to a recent stable one (like 0.8.XX).

Write the Contract:
solidity
CopyEdit
```solidity
// SPDX-License-Identifier: MIT
pragma solidity ^0.8.18;

contract SimpleStorage {
    uint256 private storedNumber;

    // Event to emit when number changes
    event NumberChanged(uint256 newNumber);

    // Function to set the number
    function setNumber(uint256 _num) public {
        storedNumber = _num;
        emit NumberChanged(_num);
    }

    // Function to get the number
```

```solidity
    function getNumber() public view returns (uint256) {
        return storedNumber;
    }
}
```

2.
   - We define a state variable `storedNumber` to hold a uint256.
   - `setNumber` updates the state and emits an event for logging.
   - `getNumber` reads the state (marked view, meaning it doesn't cost gas if called externally as it doesn't change state).
   - We specify a license identifier and solidity version for best practices.
3. **Compile the Contract:**
   - In Remix, go to the "Solidity Compiler" tab, select 0.8.18 (or match the pragma), and click "Compile SimpleStorage.sol". Any errors will show; fix if any (shouldn't have in this simple code).
   - If successful, you get a green checkmark.
4. **Deploy to a Test Network:**
   - Make sure MetaMask is on the same testnet you want to deploy to (e.g., Goerli or the "Remix VM (London)" which is an in-browser emulator if you just want quick test without a real network).
   - In Remix, go to "Deploy & Run Transactions" tab.
   - Under "Environment", select "Injected Provider – MetaMask" to deploy via your MetaMask (which should be connected to e.g. Goerli). It will ask to connect Remix to MetaMask.
   - Choose the contract "SimpleStorage" in the dropdown.

- Hit "Deploy". MetaMask pops up asking for gas fee to deploy (on Goerli, this might be something like 0.001 ETH).
- Confirm, then watch the Remix console. After a bit, you'll see the deployed contract address appear.

5. **Interact with the Deployed Contract:**
    - In Remix, under "Deployed Contracts", you'll see your contract instance and its address. It will list the functions:
        - `setNumber` and a textbox to input `_num`.
        - `getNumber` and a button.
    - Click `getNumber` right now, it should return 0 (default value).
    - In the `_num` box for `setNumber`, enter 42 and click the `setNumber` button.
    - MetaMask pops up – this is a state-changing tx. Confirm it.
    - After it's mined (Remix will show a check and event log), click `getNumber` again. Now it returns 42.
    - You have successfully written and interacted with a smart contract on a blockchain!

6. **Understanding Gas and Deployment:**
    - Check the transaction on Etherscan (testnet explorer). The contract creation transaction will show how much gas was used (maybe around 60k gas, costing ~0.00006 ETH if base fee is ~1 gwei on testnet).
    - Note that storing data cost gas (writing `storedNumber` cost 20k gas to initialize storage).
    - Each subsequent `setNumber` call costs gas (storing a new number in storage, plus some for emitting the event). The event allows off-chain tools to catch changes; on Etherscan you could see the event logs showing "NumberChanged: 42".

7. **Deploying to Mainnet or other chains:**

- The process is identical but requires real ETH for gas. Typically you'd test thoroughly on testnets and maybe get an audit for more complex contracts before mainnet deployment.
- Many use scripts (Hardhat or Truffle) for deployment in a reproducible way, especially if deploying multiple contracts or needing to verify on Etherscan.

8. **Verifying Contracts:**
    - It's good practice to verify the source code on Etherscan after deploying, so others can audit what code is at that address. Etherscan verification can be done by providing the source and compiler settings (Remix can auto-verify if using certain plugins or just manually copy code to Etherscan's verify interface).

Now you've done the basics of DApp development: written Solidity, deployed a contract, and interacted with it through a UI (Remix's UI, but conceptually similar to any web UI calling a contract).

Launching a DAO (Aragon) *(Intermediate)*

Suppose you have a community or project and want to create a DAO for governance. We'll use **Aragon** as an example because it provides a simple UI to set up a DAO (and it's mentioned in references aragon.org).

1. **Access Aragon DAO App:**
    - Visit the Aragon app (e.g., `app.aragon.org` or the new Aragon client).
    - Connect your wallet (MetaMask). Choose the network (Aragon supports Ethereum, Polygon, etc. – you might try Polygon to avoid high gas on Ethereum for practice).
2. **DAO Setup Steps (using Aragon client):**
    - **Choose Template:** Aragon might offer templates, e.g., Company, Membership, or Token-based DAO futurelearn.com.

- - *Company* (share-based) DAO: for closed groups where members join by invitation and capital.
    - *Token-based* DAO: open, anyone holding a token can vote.
  - Let's say we choose *Token-based* (permissionless membership via an ERC-20 token).
  - **DAO Name:** Enter a name, e.g., "MyExampleDAO". This might also create an ENS subdomain (on Ethereum mainnet Aragon offered .aragonid.eth names).
  - **Governance Token Setup:**
    - Decide token name, symbol, and initial supply distribution. If you already have a token contract, Aragon can use it; otherwise it can create a new token for the DAO.
    - For test, create a token "ExampleToken" symbol "EXM". Initial supply 1000 EXM. You can allocate these to founding members' addresses (e.g., give yourself 600, friend 400).
  - **Voting Parameters:** Set the voting rules:
    - Support %: minimum percentage of votes in favor for a proposal to pass (of those who voted).
    - Quorum %: minimum percentage of total token supply that must participate for vote to be valid.
    - Vote duration: how long voting stays open (e.g., 3 days).
    - For example, we might set Support 60%, Quorum 20%, Duration 48 hours for quicker decisions.
  - **Permissions:** By default, Aragon will configure that only proposals that pass can perform certain actions (like spending funds from the DAO's vault). It

basically sets up the DAO's internal governance rules automatically.
    - Review settings.
3. **Launch the DAO:**
    - Click "Create DAO". This will trigger a series of transactions:
        - One to deploy the DAO smart contracts (the kernel, token contract, voting app, finance app, etc.).
        - If on Ethereum, this can be a bit expensive (multiple contracts). On Polygon or testnet, it's cheaper.
    - Confirm each transaction in MetaMask.
    - After a short while, your DAO is live! You get a DAO address and an interface to interact (Aragon provides a web dashboard).
4. **DAO Operations:**
    - Now, in the Aragon interface, you'll see sections like "Voting", "Tokens", "Finance".
    - **Propose a Vote:** Let's say you want the DAO to spend funds (there's likely a Finance app that holds ETH or whatever currency).
        - If you provided some ETH or DAI to the DAO's vault on creation (Aragon might have let you fund it initially or you can send funds to the DAO's contract address now), you can now create a proposal: "Transfer 10 DAI to 0xFriendAddress for project expenses."
        - Fill in the parameters (recipient, amount, reference memo).
        - Submit proposal. This may just register the proposal in the DAO contract (a small transaction or it might be free if using off-chain voting with Snapshot – but assume on-chain for AragonOS).
        - Now token holders (you and friend) get to vote.

- **Voting:** Each can go to the Voting section, see the open proposal, and cast Yes or No (signing a transaction or message depending on setup).
- Because we set a 48h duration, we wait or if both of you voted yes and thresholds are met, you might be able to execute early (some systems allow early execution if outcome is mathematically decided).
- **Execution:** Once the vote passes, the Finance app contract allows execution of the transfer. You or anyone can click "Execute" which triggers the smart contract to send the 10 DAI to the friend's address.
- That's it – you've done a DAO governance cycle: propose, vote, execute.

5. **Using Snapshot (alternative off-chain voting):**
    - Some DAOs use Snapshot for voting to avoid gas fees for voters. If Aragon used on-chain, skip; but you could also configure your DAO to take Snapshot votes and then a trusted agent or a time-lock executes decisions on-chain. For learning, know that Snapshot is basically a website where token holders sign messages to vote, and those votes are counted by weight of holdings at a certain block snapshot (thus named).
    - Snapshot doesn't enforce execution; the DAO must voluntarily carry out the results. Many communities honor it by multi-sig doing what vote said, or automated if possible.

6. **Caveat:** There's a lot under the hood: Aragon deployed multiple contracts (DAO kernel, ACL, token manager, etc.). But as a DAO admin using their UI, you don't see that complexity.

7. **Exploring On-Chain:** Visit the block explorer for your network, see the contracts deployed:
    - The token contract (ERC-20) at some address (verify you got 600 EXM, friend 400 EXM as set).
    - The DAO agent/vault contract that likely holds funds.

- The voting contract where proposals are logged (you can see events for votes).
- It's instructive to see how these components work together, perhaps by reading Aragon's documentation or verified source code on explorers.

With this, you've effectively launched a mini DAO. While Aragon does heavy lifting, it aligns with how real DAOs like a protocol's DAO might operate – though many now use custom contracts or different frameworks, the principles are similar.

Building a DApp Frontend for a Smart Contract (Advanced)

For those interested in development, connecting a smart contract to a user interface is key. We'll sketch how to create a simple DApp page that interacts with the `SimpleStorage` contract we deployed.

1. **Frontend Setup:** You can use a library like **Web3.js** or **Ethers.js** to communicate with Ethereum from a web page. We'll use ethers.js as it's modern and convenient especially with MetaMask.
    - Create a basic HTML file, include a script tag for ethers (you can use a CDN or bundle via a build tool).

html
CopyEdit
```html
<!DOCTYPE html>
<html>
<head><title>SimpleStorage DApp</title></head>
<body>
    <h1>SimpleStorage DApp</h1>
    <p> Current stored number: <span id="currentValue">?</span> </p>
```

```html
    <input type="number" id="newValue" placeholder="Enter new number">
    <button id="setButton">Set Number</button>

    <script src="https://cdn.jsdelivr.net/npm/ethers/dist/ethers.min.js"></script>
    <script>
        const contractAddress = "0xYourDeployedContractAddress";
        const abi = [
            // Minimal ABI: just the functions and events we need
            "function setNumber(uint256 _num) public",
            "function getNumber() public view returns (uint256)",
            "event NumberChanged(uint256 newNumber)"
        ];

        // Connect to Ethereum provider (MetaMask injects window.ethereum)
        const provider = new ethers.providers.Web3Provider(window.ethereum);
        let contract;
        async function init() {
            await provider.send("eth_requestAccounts", []); // prompts user to connect accounts
            const signer = provider.getSigner();
```

```javascript
            contract = new ethers.Contract(contractAddress, abi, signer);

            // Fetch initial value
            const currentVal = await contract.getNumber();
            document.getElementById('currentValue').innerText = currentVal;

            // Listen to events: update value when NumberChanged
            contract.on("NumberChanged", (newNum) => {
                document.getElementById('currentValue').innerText = newNum;
            });
        }


        document.getElementById('setButton').onclick = async () => {
            const newVal = document.getElementById('newValue').value;
            try {
                const tx = await contract.setNumber(newVal);
                console.log('Transaction sent:', tx.hash);
                await tx.wait(); // wait for confirmation
```

```
                console.log('Transaction mined!');
            } catch (err) {
                console.error(err);
                alert("Transaction failed: " +
(err.message || err));
            }
        };

        init();
    </script>
</body>
</html>
```

2.
    - This script does: connect to MetaMask's provider, instantiate the contract with its ABI and address, display current stored number, and set up an event listener to update the UI when the contract emits NumberChanged.
    - The user can input a new number and click "Set Number", which calls the contract's function through the signer (MetaMask will pop up to confirm).
    - We call `await tx.wait()` to wait until mined, then console log. The event listener will update the number automatically once the event is emitted.
3. **Running the DApp:** Open this HTML file in a browser with MetaMask installed:
    - It should immediately ask to connect (due to `eth_requestAccounts` in init()).
    - After connecting, it will call `getNumber()` and display it.
    - Try setting a number: input 7, click button. MetaMask asks for confirmation (gas fee etc.). Confirm.

- On success (couple of seconds), you should see "Current stored number: 7". If you open console, you see logs of tx hash and "mined".
- If something fails (e.g., user rejects or gas too low), the catch shows an alert with error.
4. **Understanding the ABI**: We used a simplified ABI array. In practice, you could copy the ABI from Remix or compile output. Ethers.js can use this human-readable ABI format for simplicity in basic cases.
    - We included the event ABI so that `contract.on("NumberChanged")` works.
5. **React or Advanced UI:** In a real scenario, you might use a framework like React, and perhaps a library like web3-react or Ethers hooks to manage connection, and style the app nicely. The above is a barebones approach to illustrate functionality without external dependencies beyond ethers.js.
6. **Security & Deployment**:
    - If deploying such a frontend, ensure you restrict network (maybe check if `provider.network.chainId` is the expected chainId to avoid inadvertently pointing users to a malicious fork).
    - You might deploy this page on a static site hosting (GitHub Pages, Netlify, etc.) for easy sharing.

Summary of Steps: We went from contract creation to building a UI, which is exactly what many DApps are: a contract (or set of contracts) plus a web interface that calls those contracts, with users' wallets as the bridge for signing transactions.

(Exercises – Hands-On): 1. **Deploy Your Own Token:** Try deploying an ERC-20 token contract using OpenZeppelin's template through Remix. Give yourself some initial supply. Then use a block explorer's write interface or a simple web3 script to transfer some tokens to another address. *2.* **Modify the DApp:** Expand the SimpleStorage DApp to include a button that calls a function to reset the number to zero. (You'd need to add a `reset()` function to the

contract, redeploy, update ABI, etc.) *3.* **DAO Proposal Simulation:** On a testnet, simulate a DAO proposal lifecycle without Aragon: For example, deploy a simple contract that has a function `executeAction()` that does something (like toggling a boolean state), but only callable by a specific address (representing a multi-sig). Then pretend off-chain voting happened and call that function from the "DAO multi-sig" address. This exercise is more conceptual to mimic governance. *4.* **Gas Estimation:** Using the Ethers.js DApp, notice the gas it costs to call `setNumber` for different values. Does the gas usage change if you set the same number twice in a row versus a new number (hint: SSTORE opcode in Ethereum costs 20k gas for changing a storage slot to non-zero from zero, 5k if changing to another non-zero)? You can find this by looking at `tx.gasLimit` or after mining, check `txReceipt.gasUsed`. *5.* **Contribute to a Web3 Project:** Many Web3 projects are open source. Identify a project on GitHub (could be a DeFi dApp or a developer tool). Clone the repository and try to run it following their README (even if just a testnet version). Document the steps and any challenges you faced. This will give a sense of real-world Web3 dev workflows, beyond our simple examples.

Historical and Philosophical Context Revisited

To appreciate how Web3 builds on past ideas, we delve into the history of decentralization and the philosophies that underlie the movement. We also revisit key scholarly works by Dr. Justin Goldston that connect these historical threads to the current Web3 era, such as Hybrid Finance, digital inheritance, the Metaverse, and soulbound tokens.

(This section reiterates earlier historical discussion but ties explicitly to Goldston's references as requested.)

The Internet's Decentralized Roots and Cypherpunk Ideals *(Beginner)*

The concept of a decentralized web isn't entirely new:

- In the early Internet (ARPANET days), the network was designed to have no single point of failure – a packet-switching network that could survive node outages.
- **Usenet (1980s):** A decentralized discussion system, where servers distributed newsgroup posts in a peer-to-peer fashion (no central server owned all messages).
- **IRC (Internet Relay Chat):** Though there are IRC servers, the network is federated; no single company runs IRC – anyone can set one up and they link into networks.
- The **Cypherpunks** (late 80s, 90s): This community of cryptographers and programmers believed cryptography could enable privacy and individual freedom online. They popularized ideas like digital cash (e.g., David Chaum's e-cash), remailers for anonymous email, and smart contracts (Nick Szabo coined the term in 1997). They are directly the ideological ancestors of Bitcoin. Notably, a 1992 Cypherpunk manifesto stated that privacy is necessary for an open society in the electronic age, and cryptographic techniques could achieve it.
- **BitTorrent (2001):** A decentralized protocol for file sharing, exemplifying how removing central servers can make networks more robust and censorship-resistant.

Web1 had decentralized protocols (SMTP for email, HTTP for websites) but the services built on them became centralized (e.g., Gmail for email, Google Search, etc.). Web3 is a return to giving power to users via decentralized protocols but with the new tool of *blockchain consensus* to coordinate state across a distributed system of peers.

Cycles of Centralization: From Mainframes to Personal Computers to Cloud *(Intermediate)*

History often alternates:

- In computing: mainframes (central) -> personal computers (decentralized computing at user end) -> cloud (central again, with big data centers).
- In finance: gold and cash (decentralized value anyone can hold) -> centralized banking and digital money -> attempt to decentralize via Bitcoin.
- Dr. Justin Goldston in his talks and research likely notes these cycles. For instance, Web1 (decentralized content publishing) gave way to Web2 (centralized platforms) and now to Web3 (decentralizing platforms again). Goldston's *TEDxRIT 2019* talk on Web3.0 "the Blockchain Effect" pointed out how Web1 was read-only, Web2 read write, and Web3 adds read-write-own (users owning their data and assets) ted.com.

Philosophically, decentralization aligns with:

- **Libertarian ideals:** Minimizing central authority, as seen in Bitcoin's aim to be money free from government control.
- **Collectivist governance:** The paradox is decentralization can also mean collective control (the community governs via consensus). It's like a digital version of direct democracy or cooperative ownership, which historically has roots in communal decision-making structures.
- **Hobbes vs. Rousseau:** Hobbes argued for a strong central Leviathan (state) to avoid chaos; Rousseau believed in the general will of the people. Decentralized networks are more Rousseau-esque, trusting that rules can emerge from the group (encoded in smart contracts) without an absolute sovereign. Goldston's *Digital Leviathan* paper articlegateway.com plays on this Hobbesian metaphor – can a metaverse be governed by the people and not become a Leviathan? The findings suggested a balance via governance and quadruple bottom line.

Dr. Justin Goldston's Hybrid Finance (HyFi) – Bridging Old and New *(Advanced)*

In Goldston's publication *"Decentralized Finance to Hybrid Finance through blockchain: a case study of Acala and Current"* en.wikipedia.org, Hybrid Finance (HyFi) is introduced. Let's break down why this is seminal:

- **DeFi vs TradFi:** DeFi opened a parallel financial system – great for crypto-savvy users, but largely separate from traditional finance (TradFi). TradFi has scale and user trust but lacks some innovation. HyFi aims to connect them.
- **Acala-Current Case:** Current is a fintech app with millions of users (mostly not crypto users). Acala is a DeFi platform on Polkadot. Their partnership meant Current's users could access yields from Acala's DeFi seamlessly. The *first-of-its-kind* nature established a model: others can follow.
- Goldston's analysis likely highlights benefits:
    - Users get better financial products (higher interest, 24/7 markets) without needing to learn Web3 intricacies.
    - DeFi gets more liquidity and legitimacy by integrating with regulated entities.
    - It's a pragmatic approach – rather than expecting DeFi to replace banks overnight, they work together (a **synthesis** of new tech with legacy systems – hence "hybrid").
- Hybrid Finance also resonates with the idea of **CeDeFi** (centralized-decentralized finance, e.g., Binance Smart Chain – centralized validators running DeFi-like systems). HyFi is more about partnerships than technical centralization, but it recognizes a spectrum.
- The case study of Acala-Current in Goldston's work is "seminal" because it documented a blueprint soon followed by others (e.g., Revolut offering crypto, PayPal integrating crypto, etc., though those are more CeFi offering crypto rather than user funds in DeFi protocols).

- It also stresses *interoperability*: bridging blockchains with traditional databases of banks. That requires not just technical bridges but legal agreements, risk management bridging (if a smart contract fails, how does the fintech handle it for users?).

Digital Inheritance and Soulbound Tokens – Preserving Legacy *(Advanced)*

Goldston's 2023 study on digital inheritance arxiv.org using soulbound tokens (SBTs) and social recovery is pivotal:

- **Problem:** Millions in crypto have been lost when owners die without sharing keys (estates unprepared for crypto). Traditional estate laws struggle with secret keys and global assets.
- **Soulbound Tokens:** An idea by Vitalik Buterin et al., these are non-transferable tokens representing aspects of identity or affiliation (like a crypto CV, or membership badge). Goldston's case uses SBTs as a way to denote a person's planned beneficiaries or to encapsulate credentials to transfer control upon death arxiv.org.
- **Social Recovery Pallet:** On Polkadot, a pallet is a module at the runtime. Social recovery means you appoint "guardians" (friends, family) who can collectively help recover your account if you lose access (or presumably if you pass away, they could trigger a process to transfer).
- The framework likely suggests:
    - Users mint an SBT that possibly contains encrypted instructions or permissions that activate when certain conditions are met (e.g., no activity for X years or a death certificate NFT submitted by an executor).
    - The social recovery group could then help unlock the deceased's wallet to a beneficiary address, using multi-sig or threshold cryptography.
    - This keeps it decentralized (no need for a central exchange "dead man switch") but aligns with legal

needs (perhaps the SBT could even integrate legal documents or indicate the designated heir).
- Findings noted by Goldston: While this method is promising, it raises considerations (trust in guardians, privacy of estate plans, etc.) arxiv.org. Also, more research needed for edge cases (like malicious guardians, or quantum threats as mentioned).
- Why philosophical? It deals with death, legacy, and trust – age-old human issues – solved in a novel way with code and community rather than solely lawyers.

Soulbound Tokens and Identity (Goldston & Chaffer 2022)
articlegateway.com:

- They discuss how Web3 allows a digital identity that can "live forever" and accumulate assets (digital legacy). They apply **Terror Management Theory** (the idea that much human behavior is driven by subconscious fear of death) – suggesting that collecting NFTs or building an online persona that outlives you is a new way humans seek immortality.
- And **Logotherapy** (Viktor Frankl's concept of finding meaning, often through responsibility and legacy) – applying this, the act of curating a soulbound profile of achievements could be seen as meaning-making in Web3.
- It's fascinating academically: linking blockchain tokens to existential psychology and showing Web3 is not just tech; it's affecting how people think about self and legacy.

The Metaverse and Governance – The Digital Leviathan *(Advanced)*

Goldston's Bit.Country metaverse case articlegateway.com:

- It equated nation-state governance to metaverse governance. In a state, Leviathan (the government)

maintains order. In a decentralized metaverse, the community or token holders might collectively be Leviathan.
- The concept of *quadruple bottom line* mentioned means beyond profit (financial), consider social, environmental, and spiritual (or purpose) outcomes. For a metaverse, that could translate to:
    - Financial: the economy of the metaverse should be sustainable.
    - Social: users have fair representation and community benefits.
    - Environmental: maybe the platform is energy-efficient or even promotes environmental awareness in its content.
    - Existential (spiritual): the metaverse gives people a sense of meaning or belonging (which might tie to the identity SBTs again).
- The Bit.Country interviews likely revealed that people see these virtual worlds as extensions of real communities, not just games. Governance by the people (if done well) can avoid the pitfalls of centralized platforms (like Meta's metaverse could become a dystopian corporate-controlled world).
- Polkadot's role: Bit.Country on Polkadot shows how an L1 known for on-chain governance (Polkadot has sophisticated voting via DOT token) can host a metaverse that inherits those decentralization properties.

Philosophical Context:

- Linking back to the early internet ideals of cyberspace as a new frontier of freedom (John Perry Barlow's 1996 Declaration of the Independence of Cyberspace declared cyberspace free from government rule). Web3 tries to fulfill that independence through code rather than just aspiration.
- But as Goldston might caution, we must integrate interdisciplinary thinking to avoid repeating history's mistakes (e.g., ignoring law results in crackdowns, ignoring

ethics leads to scams, etc.). Hybrid and interdisciplinary methods are not just nice-to-have; they might be necessary for Web3's long-term success and societal acceptance.

(Sources from Goldston's profile were used to enrich this context: we've cited his works to show how they connect decentralization's past with present efforts.)

(Exercises – Historical/Philosophical): 1. **Compare Internet Eras:** Make a table of Web1 vs Web2 vs Web3 in terms of technology, key players, level of decentralization, and primary user benefit. (E.g., Web1: HTML/FTP, portals like Yahoo, decentralized hosting but hard to monetize; Web2: social media & cloud, FAANG companies, centralized but user-generated content boom; Web3: blockchain & p2p, protocols like Ethereum & IPFS, decentralized ownership of content/assets.) 2. **Cypherpunk Reading:** Read the Cypherpunk Manifesto (by Eric Hughes, 1993) 【no direct cite given but widely available】. Identify two predictions or statements in it that Web3 is addressing today. 3. **Hybrid Finance Debate:** Discuss with a peer (or write an essay): Is Hybrid Finance a transitional phase or the endgame? In other words, do you think eventually DeFi will fully replace TradFi (rendering HyFi moot), or will HyFi persist as the model where blockchain works behind the scenes of traditional institutions? Use Goldston's case and current trends (like banks issuing stablecoins) to argue your view. 4. **Digital Legacy Plan:** Sketch a plan using today's tools for your own digital assets in case of death. (For example: use a multi-sig wallet where 2 of 3 keys – held by spouse and close friend – are needed to move funds, and give them instructions in a will. Or use a service like Safe Haven that provides inheritance solutions on blockchain.) Compare this approach to Goldston's soulbound token concept arxiv.org – what are pros and cons of each? 5. **DAO or Leviathan?:** Consider a large platform like Facebook vs a large DAO-based platform (say a hypothetical "DeFiBook" social network on-chain). Analyze using Hobbes' perspective: would the DAO truly avoid a Leviathan (central

authority)? Or can the majority itself become a Leviathan imposing will on minorities? What mechanisms in DAO governance design could protect minority voices (ref: maybe quadratic voting or conviction voting)? Use examples from existing DAOs where applicable.

Ethical and Governance Considerations in Web3

As Web3 grows, it faces numerous ethical and governance challenges. In this chapter, we discuss regulatory landscapes around the world, dilemmas like privacy vs. compliance, the influence of politics on crypto adoption, and examine a case study of World Liberty Financial's approach to navigating these waters.

Global Regulatory Challenges *(Intermediate)*

Regulatory Spectrum: Different countries treat crypto differently:

- **Crypto-friendly havens:** El Salvador made Bitcoin legal tender (2021) – a bold move aimed at financial inclusion and attracting investment insights.som.yale.edu. While it boosted El Salvador's profile, uptake among citizens has been modest (many took the initial $30 Bitcoin bonus then not much after). It raises questions: can a country with its own currency (USD) adopt a volatile asset as currency? The experiment is ongoing. Other havens: Switzerland (clear laws, "Crypto Valley" in Zug), Singapore (welcoming but with investor protection rules), UAE (Dubai has pro-crypto zones).
- **Strict Bans:** China outright banned crypto trading and mining (2021), citing financial stability and environmental reasons. Yet they push their own CBDC (central bank digital currency). India has flip-flopped: considering a ban, then heavy tax (30% on gains) without outright ban. These moves

often come from concerns of capital flight, scams, and currency sovereignty.
- **The EU:** In 2023, the EU approved **MiCA (Markets in Crypto-Assets)** regulation atlanticcouncil.org. MiCA provides a comprehensive framework: requiring crypto service providers to register, stablecoin issuers to hold reserves and possibly cap usage, exchanges to have safeguards, etc. It basically integrates crypto into existing financial regulatory perimeter, bringing consumer protection and market integrity rules. This clarity is expected to attract businesses (passporting across EU).
- **The US:** A patchwork approach. The SEC treats many tokens as unregistered securities (leading to enforcement actions, like against Ripple's XRP and various ICOs). The CFTC views Bitcoin and Ether as commodities. There's no single crypto regulatory framework yet, leading to **regulation by enforcement** where agencies sue projects one by one, creating a chilling effect. However, political momentum is building for laws (several bills in Congress, e.g., the Lummis-Gillibrand Responsible Financial Innovation Act). The 2024 Republican platform explicitly opposes heavy crypto crackdown blockworks.co, indicating this has become a partisan issue to some extent.
- **Emerging economies:** Some, like Nigeria, saw massive crypto adoption (people using stablecoins or Bitcoin to hedge local currency inflation). Governments are torn: Nigeria tried banning banks from touching crypto, but usage went on via P2P. Many countries explore CBDCs to offer a state-controlled digital alternative.

Compliance vs Decentralization Dilemma:

- Regulators want KYC/AML (know-your-customer / anti-money-laundering) compliance to prevent illicit use. Decentralized protocols typically have no built-in KYC (a Uniswap or Aave can be accessed by anyone with a wallet).

There's a philosophical clash: crypto's openness vs. legal requirement to curb crime.
- Potential solutions: *regulated DeFi pools* – e.g., Aave Arc requires whitelisted (KYC'ed) addresses to participate, aimed at institutions. Or *identity protocols*: if there was a decentralized identity that could attest "user is not sanctioned and is over 18" without revealing identity, that could reconcile some issues. Projects like PolygonID and zkKYC ideas try this with zero-knowledge proofs.
- Privacy coins (Monero, Zcash) face delisting on exchanges due to regulator pressure, because completely private transactions worry regulators about money laundering. Some countries (Japan, Australia) have banned exchanges from offering privacy coins. Yet, advocates argue financial privacy is a human right (citing that cash provides anonymity too).
- Travel Rule: There's now guidance that crypto transfers above certain amount should include identifying info of sender/receiver (similar to bank wires). Complying with this in decentralized context is hard. Exchanges and custodians can handle it, but self-custody wallets cannot without adding metadata to transactions, which the protocols don't support widely.

Security and Consumer Protection:

- Scams and hacks are prevalent. Regulators feel pressure to protect consumers from rug pulls, Ponzi schemes, and outright theft. This leads to warnings (UK's FCA frequently warns about crypto risks, India's government ran an ad campaign against crypto investing).
- On the other hand, over-regulation can stifle innovation or push it underground. Balance is needed: e.g., requiring clear disclosure for crypto projects (to fight false advertising) might be good, but requiring every DeFi user to get a license is not feasible.

- Some jurisdictions have special sandboxes or licenses: e.g., New York's BitLicense (often criticized as onerous), or Wyoming's crypto-friendly laws (DAO LLC law, special bank charters for crypto custodians).

Ethical Dilemmas *(Advanced)*

Decentralization vs Accountability:

- If "code is law," what if code does something harmful? The DAO hack 2016: code allowed a drain; the Ethereum community faced an ethical choice – stick to "code is law" (which Ethereum Classic did, letting the hacker keep funds) or intervene for perceived justice (Ethereum forked to restore funds). Ethereum's choice was pragmatic but some said it violated immutability principles.
- Ongoing: if a DeFi protocol is exploited, should developers ever intervene (if they have admin keys or can push an update)? Many have time-locks or even renounced control to be truly decentralized. The ethical line is fuzzy: intervene to protect users vs adhere to decentralization ethos. Perhaps an intermediate: build more safeguards in code beforehand (like pausable contracts or circuit breakers).

Democratization vs Technocracy:

- Web3 claims to democratize finance, but in practice, technical and financial barriers mean a small elite often benefits most (e.g., whales and early adopters yield farming massive rewards, while late retail arrivals may lose money). Is Web3 really empowering the masses or creating a new aristocracy of insiders and tech-savvy?
- Efforts like fair launches, airdrops to users (not just VCs), etc., try to widen distribution. But one might argue, as some have, that Web3 can replicate inequality from Web2 if not careful. Ethically, projects are starting to think about **progressive decentralization** – i.e., begin somewhat

centralized to steer project, then gradually distribute power to the community when it's ready, to avoid both extremes of plutocracy and chaos.

Environmental Ethics:

- Proof-of-Work's energy use was a huge ethical debate. Bitcoin miners argue they often use excess renewable energy and provide grid stability by being flexible load, but environmentalists and some investors saw PoW as unsustainable. Ethereum's switch to PoS in 2022 cut its energy by ~99.95%, which was widely praised (and removed a talking point against Ethereum in regulatory discussions).
- That leaves Bitcoin – some institutional investors avoid it due to ESG (environmental, social, governance) concerns. On the other side, mining companies are incentivized to use cheap renewables, so in some cases they help fund renewable projects (but not always).
- Ethically, should energy be used for this? It's subjective – is securing a global decentralized value network a valid use of energy? Bitcoin proponents compare it to the energy used by gold mining or the banking system, claiming Bitcoin is more efficient in some ways. The debate continues.

Political Influence on Adoption:

- Politicians endorsing or condemning crypto can significantly influence public adoption. For example, when President Trump called Bitcoin a scam in 2019, it added stigma among some conservatives. Now with him launching NFTs and WLF, his base might warm up to crypto.
- In the US, pro-crypto politicians span both sides but recently more Republicans (like Senator Cynthia Lummis or Florida Governor DeSantis pushing pro-Bitcoin legislation) have embraced it, framing it as innovation and personal freedom. Democrats are split – some support (NYC Mayor Adams, Colorado Governor Polis accepting tax in crypto), others

- worry about consumer protection and climate (Senator Elizabeth Warren is a notable crypto skeptic).
- Globally, places with unstable currencies (Argentina, Turkey, Nigeria) see populace-led adoption. If a populist pro-crypto candidate like Milei in Argentina wins on a platform including embracing crypto, that accelerates adoption at national scale. But it could conflict with central bank policies.
- **World Liberty Financial's approach** as an example: They are proactively trying to engage regulators and institutions (with the token reserve and alliances) to show they're not a renegade operation. Possibly they aim to shape favorable regulation by being an example of "responsible innovation". Yet, the heavy political ties mean if political winds change or scandal hits those figures, it could backfire on the project and by extension color perceptions of crypto.

World Liberty Financial Case in Ethics/Governance:

- Combining personal political fundraising with a DeFi project is uncharted. If WLFI token sales were in effect raising money that eventually benefits a political campaign, that might bypass election laws. They have to navigate that carefully to avoid legal issues. If they keep it separate (it's a for-profit business venture only), then the ethical question is conflict of interest – will Trump's policy positions be driven by his financial interest in WLF? That's problematic in public service ethics.
- WLFI's token holders governance: If ordinary people bought WLFI believing in Trump and crypto, and say it doesn't perform or decisions favor insiders (like Sun or the Trumps), it could disillusion a lot of newcomers. So WLF has a responsibility to its community to be transparent and fair, lest it reinforce negative stereotypes (like "crypto is a grift").
- There's also geopolitical angle: Justin Sun (a Chinese citizen, though global businessman) investing in a Trump venture could raise eyebrows. Crypto often creates odd bedfellows – which can be great for global cooperation, but

also might attract regulatory scrutiny (Sun has had his run-ins with SEC too). They must ensure compliance thoroughly because any wrongdoing would be high-profile.

The Role of World Liberty Financial (Analysis) *(Advanced)*

Having covered WLF's specifics earlier, now put it in context:

- **Impact on Adoption:** WLF, by involving a former US President, has likely introduced crypto to demographics that were previously uninterested (e.g., older or more conservative audiences). Even if some entered via a "Trump token" hype, they now have wallets and some basic knowledge. This broadening of the user base can be positive.
- **If Successful:** If WLF grows legitimately into a robust DeFi platform with millions of users, it could pressure US regulators to finally provide clearer laws (so as not to stifle an American-led initiative). It might also inspire other politicians or large enterprises to create their own platforms (imagine an Amazon or Walmart token ecosystem – mainstream companies might jump in if a Trump-backed project showed traction).
- **If Failed or Scandalized:** Conversely, if WLF is hit with scandal (like mismanagement or It becomes a ghost project if Trump attention wanes), it could be cited by opponents as "see, even this high-profile crypto venture flopped, crypto is just speculation".
- **World Liberty Financial's governance** decisions (like that token reserve investing in Tron, ETH, etc.) effectively make it a quasi-hedge fund or ETF. If they succeed in stabilizing their ecosystem token via that reserve, it sets a model for other stablecoin or token issuers: a basket reserve (like how Libra/Diem initially planned a basket backing).
- **Ethics:** There's also conflict-of-interest ethics: WLF invests in Tron heavily right after Sun invests in WLF – that looks

like quid pro quo. In traditional finance, such insider dealings would be carefully watched or restricted. In crypto, rules are less clear, but if WLF is US-based, regulators might treat WLFI token as a security and scrutinize such moves for insider trading or market manipulation. WLF will need strong compliance advisors to avoid crossing lines (like doing a token buyback benefiting certain holders, etc., could attract class action lawsuits from other holders if not done transparently and fairly).

Future Governance and Politics:

- We may see **DAO lobbies** – groups like Coin Center already advocate for crypto in DC, maybe DAOs themselves will contribute to political campaigns to support crypto-friendly candidates (some have via community votes to donate to advocacy groups).
- On-chain governance could interface with legal governance: e.g., a city government might integrate a DAO for local decisions (there was an experiment in Decentraland where a physical land in Wyoming was governed by a DAO of NFT holders).
- **Ethical use cases:** Beyond financial, Web3 can address things like censorship-resistance (helping dissidents), economic empowerment via micro-payments, etc. The ethics of ensuring access (like making dApps usable for people with disabilities, or ensuring women in patriarchal societies can control their finances via crypto) are another dimension. Web3 can be a tool for social good, but it can also exacerbate problems if not careful (like enabling new forms of fraud or black markets).
- It's a space where **law, ethics, and code intersect** heavily. Lawyers and ethicists are now engaging with devs – something Goldston's interdisciplinary push encourages.

(Exercises – Ethics/Governance): 1. **Regulatory Roleplay:** Imagine you are a regulator tasked with drafting sensible crypto regulation.

Write a brief outline addressing: (a) consumer protection (what minimum standards exchanges or issuers should follow), (b) anti-fraud (how to deal with rug pulls or DeFi hacks – perhaps mandatory audits or reserve requirements), (c) innovation safe harbor (how to allow startups to experiment without heavy compliance for first 1-2 years unless they hit certain size). 2. **Debate Privacy:** Argue both sides of privacy coins: one side – they are essential for individual privacy and comparable to the privacy of cash; the other side – they too easily facilitate crime and should be restricted. Consider compromise solutions (like allowing them but requiring users to reveal identity to regulators if suspected of crime – though that's hard without breaking encryption). 3. **Energy Math:** Research the current estimated energy usage of Bitcoin (in TWh per year) and compare it to one or two industries (e.g., residential lighting in the US, or global aviation). Does the comparison change your perspective on whether Bitcoin's usage is "worth it"? (Cite sources). Also, what percent of Bitcoin mining is from renewable energy according to recent studies? 4. **Governance Attack Thought Experiment:** Suppose in a DeFi DAO, a malicious actor accumulates 51% of the governance token. What misdeeds could they do (e.g., vote to drain treasury to their wallet)? If the community recognizes the attack after the vote but before execution, what recourse do they have if any? Relate this to a potential real case (some smaller DAOs have had issues with governance attacks). Discuss whether some centralized fallback (like an emergency pause by founders) is ethically justified to prevent theft, or if that undermines the DAO's legitimacy. 5. **Political Influence Survey:** List at least three politicians (from any countries) who have publicly supported crypto and three who have opposed it or expressed skepticism. What reasons do they give? (e.g., support: innovation, financial inclusion, freedom; oppose: fraud, investor harm, climate). How do you think political actions (like El Salvador's Bitcoin adoption, or China's ban) have influenced the global narrative on crypto?

AI Integration and Future Predictions

Finally, we look at the synthesis of Web3 with cutting-edge technologies like artificial intelligence, and project future trends. We examine how Gemach's intelligent agents exemplify AI in Web3 today, and incorporate insights from Dr. Justin Goldston's 2019 foresight into where blockchain and quantum computing may take us in the next decade.

AI in Web3: From Gemach's Agents to Autonomous DAOs *(Advanced)*

Artificial Intelligence and Web3 are converging in multiple ways:

- **Intelligent Trading Agents:** As we saw with Gemach DAO's Alpha Intelligence docs.gemach.io, AI bots can manage crypto assets autonomously. This could extend to not just trading, but providing liquidity, arbitraging between platforms, or optimizing yield across protocols (so-called "yield farming robo-advisors"). These agents can react in milliseconds, far faster than human decision loops, potentially leading to a very AI-driven DeFi market in the future.
- **AI DAOs (DAOst):** Consider DAOs where members are not just humans but AI agents representing humans or themselves. For example, a user could deploy an AI that votes in DAO proposals on their behalf based on their preferences (essentially automated governance participation). More radically, an AI could hold tokens and participate for its own goals (there was a concept of a "plantoid" – a plant-like sculpture that is an AI-driven DAO that raises funds to self-replicate).
- **Content Creation and NFTs:** AI is generating art (e.g., DALL-E, Stable Diffusion). Coupling this with Web3, we have NFT collections partly or wholly created by AI. In future, AI could manage intellectual property rights via smart contracts – e.g., an AI musician releasing songs as NFTs, earning and reinvesting proceeds into improving its music (an autonomous artist).

- **Blockchain for AI Data & Compute:** On the flip side, Web3 can help AI: distributed computing projects (like Golem, Fetch.ai) aim to create marketplaces for computing power or data, which AI needs. Using tokens, participants can contribute GPU power or datasets and get rewarded, decentralizing the AI training process that's currently dominated by big tech.
- **AI for Security:** AI can help secure Web3 by detecting anomalies (fraudulent transactions, security breaches) faster. Imagine an AI monitoring a protocol and pausing it if it detects an exploit pattern.
- **Gemach's pioneering** is likely a harbinger: As more people trust AI agents with funds, we might see entirely autonomous hedge funds on blockchain – protocols where you just deposit funds and AI allocates across a portfolio of DeFi investments. Unlike traditional quant funds, these could be transparent (the strategies or at least the on-chain moves are visible).
- However, **risks** include: AI making unforeseen correlated decisions (flash crashes if many bots sell simultaneously), new kinds of AI-driven attacks (one AI trying to trick another – adversarial examples in trading, etc.).

Integration Challenges:

- AI usually requires off-chain processing (machine learning models), so bridging off-chain AI with on-chain action is a challenge. Oracles can bring data or AI outputs on-chain securely.
- Explainability: AI decisions can be a black box. In finance, lack of explainability has regulatory and trust issues. Perhaps recording key AI decisions on-chain (with supporting data) could help audits or trust.
- Goldston's concept of *Incentivized Symbiosis* arxiv.org touches on AI and humans cooperating via Web3 social contracts. For instance, a DAO could set rules that AI must

follow certain ethical constraints (like Asimov's laws encoded in smart contracts?).

Looking forward, one could envision:

- **Personal AI Economies:** Each person has an AI avatar that can earn money for them in the metaverse (do tasks, create content). That avatar holds a crypto wallet, signs contracts (with cryptographic keys). It might negotiate with other AIs for services. All that would utilize Web3 frameworks for trust (the AIs might not trust each other's word, but they trust the blockchain for enforcement of agreements).
- **AI Governance of Networks:** Some protocols might become so complex that AI is used to propose parameter changes (like an AI noticing a better interest rate model for a lending pool and proposing it via governance, which humans then approve). Eventually, routine decisions might be just automated (like an AI governor adjusting protocol parameters continuously similar to an algorithmic central bank).
- This raises governance and ethical questions: do we allow AI to directly control funds beyond certain limit? Should there always be a human check (perhaps a multi-sig with humans and an AI agent as signers)?

Quantum Computing and Web3's Future *(Advanced)*

We covered the threats of quantum to current crypto. Now envision Web3 in a post-quantum world, say 15-20 years out:

- All major blockchains have upgraded to PQC for signatures (likely lattice-based or hash-based cryptography). This was a huge migration, possibly done with careful planning. Perhaps multi-algorithm addresses exist for backward compatibility.
- Quantum cryptography (like QKD) might be used for layer-0 network security between nodes (ensuring communications

between data centers running nodes are eavesdrop-proof beyond classical means).
- **New cryptographic primitives:** Quantum computers might enable new things too – e.g., quantum-secure multi-party computation at scale, allowing privacy-preserving smart contracts that even outdo current ZK-SNARKs in capability.
- Or possibly **quantum tokens** – for example, using quantum states to represent value that can't be duplicated due to no-cloning theorem (this is speculative and requires quantum internet infrastructure).
- If large quantum computers exist, they might also serve as miners in some new type of consensus that uses a mix of classical and quantum proofs. Perhaps a "Proof-of-Quantum-Work" where solving some quantum algorithm puzzle yields blocks (though if QC is concentrated, that could centralize mining again).
- **Goldston's TEDx insights:** In 2019, he mentioned quantum computing as an emerging tech alongside blockchain and AI thinkers360.com. He likely anticipated that while quantum posed a risk, it also is part of the next wave of tech that blockchain will integrate with. His talks had an optimistic tone about blockchain improving everyday life ted.com – he foresaw things like supply chain tracking and secure medical records via blockchain to reduce errors. By 2025, some of these are happening: e.g., IBM and others use blockchain for food supply chain traceability (Walmart uses it for lettuce trace-back to reduce foodborne illness risk).
- Another Goldston prediction: he emphasized Web3 as not far-off, "not-too-distant future" improvements. Indeed, in a few years since 2019, we've seen NFT mainstreaming, companies like Nike and Adidas doing Web3 projects, etc. This matches that vision.

Future Predictions:

- **Mass Adoption:** In a decade, using blockchain might be as invisible and common as using internet protocols. People

may not say "I'm using a blockchain app," just like people don't say "I'm using HTTP" – it's just an app that under the hood uses blockchain for some features (ownership, micro-payments, authentication).
- **Metaverse & Web3 Merge:** The Metaverse (immersive internet) likely will use Web3 for asset ownership (your avatar skins as NFTs, etc.). If big tech dominates the metaverse, they might attempt walled gardens, but user demand for interoperability could push them to adopt Web3 standards (like users preferring games where they truly own items).
- **DAO Governments:** Perhaps small communities or even city governments adopt DAO models for certain decisions, with citizens holding tokens representing voting power (maybe one-person-one-vote soulbound tokens, not financial tokens, to keep fairness).
- **Finance:** CBDCs might coexist with decentralized stablecoins. Maybe by 2030s, people routinely hold a mix: some gov CBDC for salary, some Bitcoin as digital gold, some DeFi stablecoins for yield. Finance gets more pluralistic.
- **Challenges:** Web3 might trigger new kinds of systemic risks (flash loan attacks bridging to traditional finance – e.g., if a DeFi crash can cascade into fiat markets if they're linked via HyFi). Regulators will refine tools; we might see global coordination on crypto standards if it becomes integral to economies.
- **Green Web3:** By then, hopefully nearly all Web3 tech is running on renewable energy and efficient consensus, making the environmental argument mostly moot.
- **Social Impact:** Ideally, blockchain and AI together could provide scalable solutions for identity (e.g., refugees having a blockchain identity recognized globally), for micro-entrepreneurship (AI + Web3 micro-businesses).
- But dystopias are possible too (like total surveillance via CBDCs or deepfake AI content plus immutable records used maliciously). It's up to how we guide tech ethically now.

Dr. Goldston's research and talks encourage anticipating these futures. In his multiple TEDx talks in 2019, he essentially was telling general audiences that blockchain and associated tech would *"positively change our everyday lives"* ted.com in areas beyond finance – supply chains, healthcare, etc. We see initial evidence: e.g., IBM's Food Trust blockchain is used by large retailers, and Ethiopia uses a blockchain system (Cardano-based) to track student academic records securely (tamper-proof credentials).

In concluding:

- Web3's promise is immense, but fulfilling it requires bridging to AI, embracing quantum safety, and above all, keeping a human-centric approach (tech serving people, not just speculation).
- The textbook knowledge we've assembled is just the beginning. The reader, armed with both conceptual understanding and practical skills, can now be a part of shaping this Web3 future.

(Exercises – Future Predictions): 1. **Envision 2035:** Write a short scenario of a day in the life of someone in 2035 where Web3 and AI are ubiquitous yet seamless. For example: they wake up in a home which is part of a DAO-owned community, get into a self driving car they co-own via NFTs, their personal AI handles paying tolls via crypto wallet, they work in a metaverse with colleagues worldwide earning in stablecoins, etc. Try to include at least 5 distinct Web3 or AI elements that we discussed. 2. **AI DAO Brainstorm:** Design a concept for a DAO that has an AI as a member or officer. What would the AI's role be? (Perhaps "Treasurer AI" that optimizes investments, or "Moderator AI" that filters proposal spam.) What safeguards would you need so that human members trust the AI and the AI doesn't exceed its authority? 3. **Quantum Crisis Drill:** Imagine it's announced that a quantum computer has broken Bitcoin's elliptic curve. What immediate steps should the Bitcoin community and exchanges take in the following weeks to protect funds? (E.g., encourage moving to new multi-sig addresses based

on new algorithms, pausing some services, etc.) And how might markets react (likely price volatility)? *4.* **Interdisciplinary Team:** If you were starting a Web3 project today aimed at, say, decentralized healthcare record management, what experts would you include in your team aside from blockchain developers? List at least 5 different specialties (e.g., legal, medical informatics, UX design, cryptography, etc.) and briefly say what each contributes to ensure the project's success and compliance. *5.* **Measures of Success:** What metrics would indicate that Web3 has achieved Goldston's vision of positively changing everyday life? Propose 3-5 measurable indicators for 2030 (for instance: percentage of world population using a self-custodial crypto wallet, number of countries with >50% of supply chains using blockchain for provenance, reduction in unbanked population due to Web3 solutions, etc.). How close are we to any of those metrics today?

Conclusion: Embracing the Web3 Future

Web3 represents a paradigm shift as significant as the advent of the World Wide Web itself. It merges technological innovation with economic and social reimagination:

- It challenges us to think in terms of **systems** – connecting technical protocols with legal frameworks, market incentives, and human behavior.
- It redistributes power, giving individuals direct control over assets, identity, and even the platforms they use through governance tokens.
- It's still early, with **many challenges** to overcome (scalability, usability, regulatory integration, security against evolving threats), but the pace of improvement is rapid.

In this textbook, we:

- Traveled from the basics of blockchains and smart contracts through advanced DeFi mechanisms and DAO governance, adopting multiple perspectives for different readers.

- Analyzed **real case studies** like Gemach DAO, which blends AI with DeFi in a community-centric way, and World Liberty Financial, illustrating the interplay of crypto with global personalities and politics.
- Ensured mathematical rigor by examining the algorithms and cryptography that make trustless systems possible, and even looking at the equations governing DeFi markets and consensus security.
- Wove in historical context and philosophy, from the cypherpunk movement to modern research on digital society by Dr. Justin Goldston and peers, to show that Web3 is part of a continuum of humanity's quest for better ways to organize and empower ourselves.
- Addressed ethical issues and the need for good governance, because technology alone doesn't create a utopia – it's how we choose to implement and use it.

Dr. Justin Goldston's 2019 foresights have largely been validated:

- He predicted blockchain would permeate daily life positively ted.com – indeed, blockchain is behind more and more mainstream applications (though sometimes unbeknownst to users). His example of near error-free medical records is being piloted in places (Estonia's e-health system uses blockchain tech for audit trails).
- He anticipated the convergence of blockchain with AI and quantum computing thinkers360.com – as we discussed, this convergence is happening, and preparing for it is a focus of cutting-edge research. His emphasis on *fast-paced emerging technologies* reminds us that continuous learning is essential in this space thinkers360.com.

Empowering the Reader: We structured content for different expertise levels so that:

- A beginner should now grasp what Web3 is and why it matters, and even be able to perform simple actions like sending crypto or using a dApp.
- An intermediate learner can delve into writing smart contracts, understand how DeFi protocols function and perhaps contribute to a DAO.
- An advanced professional has reference material on cryptographic proofs, algorithmic details, and an understanding of how to scale and secure systems – enabling them to engineer more robust platforms.
- A researcher finds pointers to key literature and a holistic framework (systems thinking) to approach open problems – perhaps inspiring the next thesis or product idea that will push Web3 forward.

The Web3 space is collaborative and open, much like this textbook cites open research and uses open-source knowledge. We encourage you to get involved:

- Try out platforms, contribute to forums or GitHub repositories of projects you're passionate about.
- Experiment with building – whether it's a small Solidity contract or a full dApp. The exercises in this book are starting points for deeper projects.
- Join a DAO or a local Web3 meetup to discuss and learn collectively; the community is one of Web3's greatest assets.

Future outlook highlights:

- Expect user experience to dramatically improve – Web3 apps will become as easy to use as web2 apps today, abstracting away wallet quirks and seed phrases (possibly via social recovery, better UX, or even hardware secure enclaves in phones).
- Regulatory clarity will likely increase investment and participation by traditional institutions, but decentralized alternatives will also flourish in parallel, hopefully finding a

healthy coexistence (Hybrid Finance as Goldston described current.com).
- New jobs and roles will emerge that we can't fully imagine – just as Web2 gave us social media managers and app developers, Web3 might give us community-economists (managing DAO token economies), metaverse architects, and AI wranglers for DAOs.
- The ethos of Web3 – openness, transparency, decentralization – could influence other fields. For example, open science could use blockchain for sharing and crediting research data (some initiatives already do, e.g., blockchain for clinical trial data integrity).

In closing, *Welcome to Web3* – not just as the title of this textbook, but as an invitation: This new web is being built **right now**, and it needs builders, thinkers, critics, and users of all kinds. By understanding the principles and challenges laid out in this book, you are better equipped to shape Web3's evolution responsibly and creatively.

Web3 promises a future where technology serves to **augment human freedom, trust, and collaboration on a global scale**, much as the internet once promised to connect us. Realizing that promise is the work of our generation of technologists, policymakers, and citizens. With knowledge, critical thinking, and ethical action, we can ensure that Web3 develops into a truly **inclusive, secure, and empowering Web** for all.

Good luck on your Web3 journey – the decentralized future is yours to help build!

Made in the USA
Columbia, SC
20 June 2025